LOCOMOTION PAPERS

Lincolnshire Loop Line (GNR) and the River Witham

by
A.J. Ludlam

THE OAKWOOD PRESS

© Oakwood Press and A.J. Ludlam, 1995

British Library Cataloguing-in-Publication Data
A record for this book is available from the British Library
ISBN 0 85361 464 4

Typeset by Oakwood Graphics

Printed by Henry Ling Ltd, Dorchester

Above: An engraving of 1857, showing Clayton and Shuttleworth Stamp End Works, in Lincoln. The firm was world famous for threshing machinery and by 1906 laid claim to a total of 98,000 machines. From about 1820 onwards a Clayton's Witham steam packet service sailed from the wharf to Boston.

Front Cover: Class 'K3' 2-6-0 No. 61948 with a Doncaster to Peterborough train at Langrick station on 14th March, 1953. *Les Perrin*

Title Page: The elaborate wooden bridge across the River Witham at Bardney, October 1848. *Illustrated London News*

Other Oakwood Press books by the same author:
  Catterick Camp Military Railway and the Richmond Branch
  The East Lincolnshire Railway
  Horncastle & Woodhall Junction Railway
  Louth, Mablethorpe and Willoughby Loop Line
  RAF Cranwell Railway
  Spilsby to Firsby Railway (out of print)
Written with W.B. Herbert:
  Louth to Bardney Branch

Published by, The Oakwood Press, P.O. Box 122, Headington, Oxford

Contents

Maid of all work class 'J6' 0-6-0 No. 64247 passes Calders, Boston with the 9.39 am Boston to Peterborough train, summer 1956. *Les Perrin*

The tall building with the covered way jutting out ot the side of Brayford pool on the east wharf was the bonded warehouse of the GNR, which had not long been open when this view was taken in the early 1900s.

Author's Collection

Introduction

'And for you that have heard many grave, serious men pity Anglers, let me tell you, Sir, there be many men that are taken by others to be serious and grave men, whom we condemn and pity.'

Izaak Walton

The Fens, which occupy the area of land through which the majority of the Lincolnshire Loop line passed, form a prominent feature of the Lincolnshire landscape. The drainage of the fenlands was an ongoing human industry since the time of the Romans. After the Norman invasion, steady progress was made, until the time of the Civil War, at which time the fen dwellers took advantage of the confusion caused by the conflict to repossess the land, filling in drains, destroying sluices and reducing the whole level in a short time to its original drowned state. The historian, Camden, gave this desciption of the manners and habits of the people inhabiting the fens:

> They that inhabit this fennish county were, in Saxon times, called 'Gyrvii', that is fen-men, a kind of people according to the nature of the place where they dwell, rude, uncivil and envious of others, whom they call upland man; who, stalking high upon stilts apply their minds to grazing, fishing and fowling. It is not all surprising that people thus circumstanced should be roused to opposition and outrage by operations which, if they succeeded, would cause a revolution in their established customs and destroy the whole system of their domestic economy.

Drainage of the fenlands continued, successive areas were enclosed, and upon completion of East, West and Wildmore Fens, about 60,000 acres, the race of stiltwalkers became extinct. During the first 50 years of the 19th century, up to the advent of the railways in Lincolnshire, the drainage and cultivation of the fens and marshes were greatly improved, many of the old wind-mill pumps replaced by steam engines, by which water was raised from the lower levels into the higher drains and rivers.

Few counties in England are blessed with the various gifts of nature than those bestowed on Lincolnshire. The same district affords light loamy soils for the production of corn, and green winter food, while the neighbouring marshes provided excellent pasturage for cattle and sheep in the summer. The produce of the county was principally sheep, cattle, horses and corn. There were in the early 1840s, an estimated 2,500,000 sheep in Lincolnshire, yielding about 22 million pounds of wool. Great quantities of wool were despatched to Yorkshire, the coming of the railways offered a quicker and more efficient means of transportation for this and other agricultural produce.

The River Witham has its whole course in Lincolnshire; at Lincoln it becomes navigable, flowing in a south-easterly direction to Boston and the sea, receiving in its course the numerous drains of the fens, many of which are navigable to small craft. It was along the banks of the Witham that the Great Northern Railway Company (GNR) decided to lay the greater part of its Lincolnshire Loop Line, the first part of the GNR system, wholly owned by the company, to earn revenue. The river and the railway are closely associated not only geographically, but also administratively, the GNR eventually taking over the maintenance of the river. It is because of this close association that I have decided to give a brief history of the River Witham, prior to dealing with the

Class 'B1' 4-6-0 No. 61082 of Immingham shed makes a fine sight as it leaves Boston with the 5.12 pm to Peterborough seen here at Sleaford Junction on railway.

I would refer the reader to two of my previous books (both published by The Oakwood Press), which deal with railways which joined the Loop line between Boston and Lincoln: *The Horncastle and Woodhall Junction Railway*, joined the Loop line at Woodhall Junction, (Kirkstead), and the *Louth to Bardney Branch* which joined at Bardney. Motive power at Boston is comprehensively covered in my book, *The East Lincolnshire Railway*, and is only briefly described here. The railway histories of the three major centres served by the Loop line, Peterborough, Boston and Lincoln are exhaustively covered elsewhere, so my concern here has been to try and deal with the intermediate stations between those centres.

With Lincoln cathedral in the background class 'B1' 4-6-0 No. 1193 runs light over the Witham on 14th July, 1947. The large building on the right is the LNER grain warehouse, now demolished.   *H.C. Casserley*

A map by John Grundy Jnr. of the River Witham and adjacent fens in 1762. Note the meandering course of the old river between Boston and Chapel Hill.

Chapter One

The River Witham

The River Witham rises about 10 miles north of Stamford, in Lincolnshire, near Thistleton and South Witham, at this point it is 339 ft above sea level. The river follows a circuitous course, ending at Fishtoft. The distance between the beginning and its end, as the crow flies, is 28 miles, the actual length of the river is 68 miles, from its source to Boston Deeps.

By the time the river reaches Lincoln it is a mere 16 feet above sea level, its main tributaries on this first part of its journey, the Brant and Till. After leaving Lincoln the river continues for 8 miles in an easterly direction before bending south for the final 22 miles into Boston. At this point it was once tidal and navigable for large vessels. After a final 8 miles through a trained channel it discharged into the estuary at Clayhole. Between Boston and Lincoln it was canalised and navigable for barges. The Langworth joins the Witham just below Lincoln, the Bain at Tattershall and the Slea at Dogdyke.

There is good reason to believe that the Witham was the result of the union of two streams. The Witham originally discharged into a large mere above Lincoln, so draining the River Trent. The Langworth emptied into a large mere between Washingborough and Chapel Hill, the outlet was by a tidal creek which ran from the mere through the marshes, where Boston now stands, to the sea, a further outlet probably running through the East and West Fens to Wainfleet Haven.

It is assumed that the Romans drained the swampy land lying to the north and west of Lincoln, either by deepening an existing watercourse, or cutting a line along that of Fossdyke Canal. At the same time they banked the Trent and drained the low land with the exception of the deep part of Brayford Mere.

In order to construct a canal which would allow boats to journey from the sea at Boston, to Lincoln, a cutting was made through the high ground to the east of Brayford Mere to Short Ferry, two miles below Fiskerton, and from there along the edge of the high land in an almost straight line until it joined the tidal creek near Chapel Hill. Below Chapel Hill, until a new cut was made in 1761, the tidal river ran a very tortuous 12 mile route.

Before the construction of the Grand Sluice, near Boston, the flow of the tide up river seldom went beyond Dogdyke or Chapel Hill. It is likely that the Romans also directed some of the water travelling down the upper Witham into Sincil Dyke which left the Witham half a mile above the city, joining it again near the site of the GNR station; this no doubt formed part of their drainage system, built to relieve the city of flooding.

After the completion of the work of joining Lincoln to the sea, via the Witham, the river became the major means of exporting corn and importing wine and goods from abroad. Larger sea-going vessels would lie in the haven below Boston, or perhaps Dogdyke, and unload into smaller boats, more suitable for navigating the upper reaches of the river. The result was that the transportation of merchandise overland, which had previously been the case, when Wainfleet

1

had been the sea port for Lincoln, was eliminated.

During the reign of Henry IV, Lincoln and Boston became major import and export centres. In one year Lincoln paid £656 12s. 2d. in Quinzine duties and Boston £780 15s. 3d., compared with London's £830 12s. 10d. The wool trade was sufficiently important to warrant the construction of a dock and warehouse at Calscroft, near Sheepwash Grange, here ships belonging to Lincoln merchants loaded and discharged their cargoes; a dock was also made at Dogdyke.

With no authority charged with the upkeep of the river it began to deteriorate, resulting in a decline in trade at Lincoln; in 1369 the staple for wool was transferred to Boston. During the 15th century Abbots of the monasteries along the river were accused of neglecting to repair banks and channel.

In the reign of Henry VII a Commission decided that things could be improved if the sea water was prevented from flowing up river. It was decided to erect a sluice and floodgates at Boston. The work was carried out by dutchman May Hake, he and his men were paid at a rate of four shillings a day with a £50 gratuity on completion of the work. Fourteen stone masons and their materials were conveyed from Calais to Boston. The sluice was built in the middle of the river, connecting to land on either side. This remained the only bridge across the river until the erection of an iron structure in 1807. A stone pier 13 ft wide and almost 44 ft long was built in the centre of the river, to this the doors for excluding the tide were attached on huge iron hooks. By 1642, the gates were no longer in place and sea water was once again flowing several miles beyond Boston.

An Act, passed in the reign of Charles II, proposed improving the navigation between Boston and the River Trent, via Lincoln:

> At the present time the said navigation is much obstructed and in great decay, by reason that the river or ancient channels of the Witham and Fossdyke are much silted and landed up and thereby not passable with boats and lighters as formerly, to the great decay of trade and commerce in the said city (Lincoln), and all the market towns neare any of the said rivers; which hath produced in them much poverty and depopulation.

The Act resulted in work being undertaken to the Fossdyke but not to the Witham.

A report published in the middle of the 18th century said,

> This once flourishing river has, for many years, been falling into decay by the banks being suffered to become ruinous and incapable of sustaining and containing the water in times of high water floods, so that those floods which necessary and useful heretofore, by their velocity and weight, to cleanse out the sand and sediment brought up by tides, have been, and now are, suffered to run out of their ancient and natural course and expand over adjoining fens and low grounds, whereby those sands, for want of reflowing power of adequate force to carry them back, have now so much chocked up [sic] the Haven from Boston to the sea that for several years past navigation thereof has been lost to shipping and it is now become even difficult for barges of about thirty tons burden to get up to the town in neap tides, and for several miles above the town of Boston the said river is totally lost in so much that the bottom is, in many places, some feet higher than the adjoining low grounds . . . the flood waters lie so stagnant on the

Barges drying their sails in Brayford Mere, Lincoln, early 1900s.   *Author's Collection*

The Fossdyke links Brayford in Lincoln with the River Trent at Torksey. The swing bridge by
the Sun Hotel, at Saxilby, opens to allow a barge through.   *D.N. Robinson Collection*

land as to destroy the herbage thereof and render them not only useless and unprofitable but also extremely noxious and unwholesome to the adjacent inhabitants.

The result of the incapacity of the Witham was that most traffic went out of Lincolnshire via the Humber, Gainsborough playing an important part in this trade. During the 1700s Gainsborough had flourished as goods were transferred between sea-going and river-going vessels. The decline of the Lincolnshire ports was not helped by the shift to trade with America and Asia during the 18th century, most of this trade being carried through ports on the west side of the country.

Hull developed as the most important port on the east coast, apart from those dealing with the shipment of coal. By 1700 Hull was dealing with most of the trade carried on the Trent and from north Lincolnshire. By this time Kings Lynn had replaced Boston as the principal port on the Wash, although Boston remained the second largest town in Lincolnshire.

This was the situation at the beginning of the canal age. Lincolnshire waterways were isolated from the developing national system, the only contact with the Midlands and Yorkshire was the Fossdyke. Locks on the Fossdyke were designed to accommodate the Lincolnshire ketch, rather than the narrow boats of the Midlands. In 1740, Lincoln Corporation leased Fossdyke for 999 years to Richard Ellison of Thorne, who paid £75 per annum. The restoration of the Fossdyke was completed by Ellison's son, also Richard, at a cost in excess of £3,000. Annual incomes rose from £75 in 1740 to £2,367, in 1789. The Ellisons made a fortune and Lincoln Corporation was accused of incompetence.

Schemes were proposed for restoring the River Witham to a navigable state in 1744 and 1745, the first by John Grundy, the second by Daniel Coppin. Meetings concerned with the schemes continued into the 1750s, and Grundy was asked to present a further report. A lot of debate centred around the positioning of the sluice at Boston. Grundy had suggested that it be erected a little above Antons Gowt. Later he proposed that Hakes' structure, erected in 1500 and used since as a bridge, should be converted into a sluice. Kings Lynn engineer Langley Edwards considered that not enough water for navigation and drainage could be obtained at the bridge and that an entirely new sluice was required further up the river. He, however, agreed with the Grundy scheme in general.

In 1761 John Grundy, Langley Edwards and John Smeaton produced a joint report largely following a map drawn by Grundy in 1757, the only difference being the location of the sluice at the Boston end of the river. The new sluice was to be erected between Lodowicks Gowt and Boston bridge, it was to have three pairs of sea doors and a navigable lock, with two pairs of landward doors and one pair seaward. At the time it was possibly the largest structure of its kind built in England. A completely new channel was to be cut from the sluice to Chapel Hill, shortening the distance by 2½ miles. The Act was passed by Parliament on 2nd June, 1762.

From Chapel Hill the river was to continue in its course but was to be deepened and widened as required. One waggon bridge and two horse bridges were to cross the river and a new sluice built at Antons Gowt to facilitate the drainage of Wildmore Fen and West Fen. Three further locks were proposed between Lincoln and Boston, at Stamp End, Barlings and Kirkstead. The cost of the scheme was estimated at £45,219 9s. 5d., and work began immediately and was completed by 1770.

The Witham was divided into six drainage districts between Lincoln and Boston and a Commission set up to deal with navigation. Traffic on the river increased and the tolls at Lincoln and Boston rose from £263 in 1763 to £898 by 1790. Until 1798, the shallowness and narrowness of the Witham between Brayford Head and Stamp End, and restricted passage under High Bridge, prevented vessels sailing right through into the Fossdyke. The conveyance of merchandise from one waterway to the other provided Lincoln carters with employment, and the City Corporation with dues which they were reluctant to forego. The problem was eliminated when provision was made in the Horncastle Navigation Act of 1792 for work to be carried out to effect a connection between the Witham and the Fossdyke. The provision was in the form of a by-pass canal allowing direct access to the Trent.

Knowledge of these proposals ensured that the work required in Lincoln was carried out. The work, which included the removal of a ford close by the site of Brayford Bridge, was completed by 1795 and traffic was once again able to move between Witham and the Fossdyke.

Further improvement of the river resulted from the Witham Navigation Act of 1812, and by 1824 a channel of six feet in depth had been established between Lincoln and Boston.

High Bridge, in Lincoln, continued to cause problems for navigation; a petition, presented to the House of Lords by the Mayor, Aldermen and Burgesses of the City, in 1846, described the problem: 'The ordinary depth of water under High Bridge when it stands at the height of the datum line drawn from the weir of Stamp End lock to a mark on the bridge is three feet eight inches at most, while the depth of water in the Fossdyke, immediately above, is five feet, and in the Witham, immediately below, six feet'. The result was that vessels often had to lighten their load in order to be able to pass under the bridge.

Flood waters presented a different problem. The increase in the depth of water and the resulting decrease in headway beneath the arch of the bridge, meant that vessels sometimes had to lie up in the river below the bridge for several days. On some occasions boatmen would allow water into the holds of their vessels in order to sit them low enough in the water to avoid the arch.

The 1846 petition was also concerned with the proposals of the London and York Railway Company, at that time before Parliament. Included in this legislation were provisions for the company to take a 999 year lease on the Witham, and about 990 years on the Fossdyke. The petitioners were anxious to protect the interests of the navigation and ensure its continued maintenance.

Discussions took place between representatives of the London and York Company (soon to become the Great Northern Railway Company) and the City. In March 1846, the City Council received a report from William Cubitt, Engineer of the railway company, describing his proposals for the section of the river through High Bridge. Cubitt proposed an entirely new bridge with a width of

A group of barges unloading their cargoes outside the Lincoln Cake Mill, below Magpie Bridge about 1907.

Author's Collection

High Bridge, in Lincoln showing the restricted passage offered to river craft.

Author's Collection

The ferry across the River Witham at Five Mile House in 1925. The chain mechanism can be seen at the centre of the ferry; the two men are Dave Hewitt and George Huteson.   *Norman Clark*

30 ft, almost twice that of High Bridge. In order to facilitate the scheme the scheme the City Council would have to obtain land to the south of the river from High Bridge to Brayford. This would allow widening of the river and the installation of a continuous tow path, from Stamp End lock to Brayford Mere, as well as an increased depth of one foot.

Although the bulk of the expenses for the proposals would be provided by the railway company, Lincoln Corporation and the Trustees or Proprietors of the Fossdyke and Witham navigations would be expected to contribute £1,000 each. The new bridge was never built and boats continued to struggle through High Bridge.

The Fossdyke and Witham navigations became the responsibility of the GNR in 1846, the company taking over the rights and liabilities of the Company of Proprietors of the Witham Navigation, under a lease of 999 years; they became responsible for maintaining Bardney lock and Stamp End lock, as well as the bed of the river from Bardney lock to Brayford Mere. Their responsibility also included the Sincil Dyke and Bargate Weir sluices, the bank of the old river at Branston Island, and both banks above Bardney lock, except those bordering Washingborough and Heighington Drainage District Board, to whom the GNR paid £2,000 per annum, to discharge that part of their liability.

The Witham General Commissioners were responsibile for maintaining the bed between Grand Sluice and Bardney lock and the west bank of that length. They paid the GNR £2,800 per annum to maintain the east bank.

Improvements to the waterways allowed merchandise to travel more easily inland to the Midlands or down the coast to London. The drainage of the fenland and enclosures of commons brought about a gradual increase in arable farming and a decrease in pasture. Lincolnshire became the granary of the Midlands, Yorkshire and Lancashire. Coal was imported from Yorkshire in the first instance, and later Nottinghamshire and Derbyshire coalfields.

Boston began to prosper as produce from the surrounding areas was loaded into ships moored in the town; throughout the early 19th century it was the principal commercial town of Lincolnshire. Large granaries were built close to the haven and to the north of the town the hamlet of Witham developed around the Grand Sluice, where warehouses and coal yards were established.

At Lincoln more warehouses, coal yards and small ship yards were established at Brayford Pool, whilst the half mile riverbank between High Bridge and Stamp End developed as a wharf area.

Chapter Two

Traffic on the River Witham

Horse drawn packets began services on the Fossdyke in 1805 and on the Witham in 1809. As well as moving merchandise the boats also took passengers, travellers, and the local people going to market. 'Packet Inns', found along the route were similar in character to the old coaching inns, the Barge Inn, at Grand Sluice, Boston, and Five Mile House, near Lincoln were such establishments.

Ferries linked one river bank with the other, these were either a rowing boat or, more likely, a flat bottomed raft-like craft pulled by chains. A ferry operated at Tattershall until 1793, when an Act authorised the construction of a bridge. At Langrick a ferry was established when new cuts were made as a result of the 1861 Act. This was a flat bottomed, chain operated ferry, the last such boat built, it was made by Edward Portess, a blacksmith and wheelwright, who worked near the ferry. Horses, cattle and wagons were transported across the river on these craft, cattle often jumped overboard halfway across and swam the rest of the way.

A bridge of steel bow girder construction was thrown across the river in about 1899. A regular ferry user commented, 'There was a time when one was content to wait patiently on the distant side of the river, yelling at the top of one's voice at intervals of half-a-minute for the ferryman to appear, and, satisfied if one could get across in a quarter of an hour . . . . even when the boatman had to break the ice as he came, though that lengthened the interval in which one had to wait shivering for the vessel to reach one.'

Kirkstead ferry existed until 1891, when, at the cost of £1,000, the GNR opened a swing bridge across the river, 'for the convenience of passengers and goods going to the station there'. A commentator remarked, 'The picturesque nature of the old style has yielded to a structure that has no pretensions to beauty'. The bridge was designed by a local man, J.W. Atkinson. Charges were one penny per head for the whole day, vehicles paid one penny per wheel, there were no charges on Sunday. The bridge, freed from tolls in 1938, became increasingly more difficult to operate and was replaced by a flyover bridge in July 1968.

A ferry, established at Bardney in 1714, remained operational until 1893, when a bridge was erected at an estimated cost of £7,250, of which the GNR contributed £3,000; the rights of the ferry were bought for £777.

At Five Mile House the car ferry was replaced by a footbridge in 1957. Norman Clark, who worked at Five Mile House between 1925 and 1929, described his experiences;

In 1925 there was a vacancy for a lad porter on the railway at Five Mile House, at a wage of one pound a week, seven shillings more than I was earning as an apprentice engineer at Ruston and Hornsby, as well as the convenience of working nearer home, (Fiskerton). At that time there were two lad porters, one signalman and a station master

The approach to High Street Bridge in Lincoln, early 1900s.

on the traffic side plus four platelayers. The original station was burned down in 1919, believed to have been caused by a spark from a passing locomotive. The station master's house, office, waiting room and the signal box were destroyed. The fire was observed from the village school at about midnight, where a dance was in progress to celebrate the end of World War I. My father was one who rushed from the dance to the station to offer help, but there was little they could do. The buildings were never replaced, except for the signal box. A small hut was provided as an office and another for a waiting room. The resident station master was moved to a vacant post at Dogdyke and a single man installed at Five Mile House.

Operating the ferry boats was one of my railway duties. There were three boats. A large ferry for vehicles, a smaller one for passengers and a punt, or cob, which we sculled across the river, as occasionally the ferry was found to be on the wrong side, and it was necessary to fetch it back.

The ferries were propelled by turning a crank handle, which turned a pulley wheel over which a chain passed. The chain was stretched from bank to bank and could be tightened or slackened with a windlass. It was easy to see that the chain could be a danger to river traffic. On the approach of a barge or other river craft it was necessary to lower the chain to allow free passage over it.

The ferry was open from 6 am to 8 pm on weekdays and 8 am to 8pm on Sundays.

Washingborough had a row boat ferry across to Greetwell. Packets called at a dock there: 'There was always a great stir when the vessel came puffing up or down the river and, with much shouting and casting of ropes, made her daily call.'

A name associated with river traffic in the late 18th, early 19th centuries, was Charles West, who was born in 1767. He was apprenticed to the owner of a coastal sloop, *The Breeze*, later becoming part owner and eventually sole owner. He acquired barges for the river traffic between Lincoln and Boston.

Nathaniel Clayton also ran a service of packets between the two towns. It is likely that at that time West was based in Boston and Clayton in Lincoln. The *Stamford Mercury* appears to make the first mention of a steam powered packet on 19th August, 1813. 'There is some reason to expect that an attempt will shortly be made to render the principle of the steamboat subservient to the public convenience in this county, by means of a vessel of that description which is designed to serve as a passage boat on the River Witham between Boston and Lincoln'.

By 1814 the steam packet *Caledonia*, was working between Gainsborough and Hull. Soon afterwards quite a fleet developed, dealing with traffic between Grimsby and Hull, Barton and Hull, and later Nottingham and Gainsborough, New Holland and Hull and Lincoln to Gainsborough. The Gainsborough and Hull packet left Hull at a quarter to seven in the morning, arriving at Gainsborough at one o'clock, left for the return at three o'clock and reached Hull at ten o'clock, a distance of about 100 miles in 12 hours. In March 1815 the *Caledonia* steam packet did the trip in under 10 hours, including stoppages.

A newspaper reference, in June 1815 reported that Mr Merryweather's patent for improved means of propelling vessels was fitted to a steam packet on the Witham. On 22nd March, 1816, an advertisement appeared drawing attention to a better service offered by Nathaniel Clayton, proprietor of the packet, *Two Brothers*, Joseph Islip, of the *Off She Goes*, and Joseph Hornbuckle of the

The schooner *G.R. Berg* unloading linseed at Gainsborough.   *G. Brocklehurst*

Humber keels near Gainsborough *c.* 1920.   *G. Brocklehurst*

Commercial. It would appear that this was in anticipation of the imminent arrival of the steam packet on the Witham and the opening shot of what was to be a bitter struggle.

On the same day, the steam packet, *Witham*, was launched by Shuttleworth and Robinson from their Waterside South yard, in Lincoln. By September it was noted that she was working regularly between Lincoln and Boston. In March 1817 the boiler of the packet burst, a few miles out of Lincoln, but none of the passengers on board were injured. By the following July a further steam packet was operating the route.

Nathaniel Clayton's resentment of the steam packets made the newspapers a couple of times. Firstly, in November 1816, he placed his non-steam packet between the steamer and the hauling path and was prosecuted for breaking the byelaws of the Witham Navigation. His hatred again manifested itself in October, 1819, when he ran his packet into the *Favorite* steam packet, causing it much damage. Clayton had to pay a fine of 20 shillings and costs. The situation had changed by 1825, when there was mention of a steam packet belonging to Messrs West and Clayton. Certainly by 1826 Nathaniel Clayton was the master of the steam packet *Countess of Warwick*, which had been launched by Robinson's of Lincoln in November 1818. Mrs. Clayton organised the packet trade and purchased the steamer to augment the fleet of non-steamers, the former being more favoured by passengers. During the 1820s competition became more intense and West carried passengers free of charge, providing refreshments *en route*; he further irritated his competitors by providing a band on board his steam packets.

There were three steam packets operating the daily service between Lincoln and Boston by the mid-1820s: the *Witham*, the *Favorite* and the *Countess of Warwick*. Departing from Lincoln at 10.00 am, they arrived in Boston at 4.00 pm. Sailing packets worked from the 'Magpie Inn' to Bardney, Southrey, Tan Vats and Kirkstead and along the Fossdyke to Saxilby and Torksey from the 'Royal William', and to Gainsborough, one from the 'Black Bull' and one from Slacks Yard. From Brayford there were sailings to Gainsborough and Hull once a week and to Sheffield twice a month. Water carriage was available to many parts of the Midlands and Eastern England, and services for carrying goods along the Witham to Coningsby, Tattershall and Horncastle, from where carriers transported goods to Spilsby, Alford and the surrounding districts.

A complaint in the press in June 1835 concerned the practice of boat owners acting as factors for the sale of corn. There is no doubt that the packet owners had realised the opportunities for trading with many commodities, coal and grain in particular. They were in direct contact with the producers and consumers and controlled their own transport. John West was one who had taken up trading, he had a warehouse built on the river bank with a small wharf fitted with a crane. The building was used for the reception of freightage for the river traffic. He also had other warehouses amongst adjacent property in which he stored grain. West retired from active involvement with steam packets, selling them to others who formed the Witham Steam Packet Company. He did, however, continue to trade in grain until his death.

The first iron boat to work the Witham was built for John West by William

A fine view of Brayford in the early 1900s. Considering there were eight corn merchants, thee timber firms, a brewer, a coal merchant and an oil company, it is no wonder that barges were tied up three deep at wharf side on many occasions.

Author's Collection

Howden, of Boston, in 1836; named *Celerity*, it was expected to make the journey between Lincoln and Boston in three hours. Nathaniel Clayton junior, became its master in 1842. He had formerly worked at Butterly iron works but returned to work for his mother upon the death of his father in 1827. In 1842, with his brother-in-law, Joseph Shuttleworth, Clayton set up Stamp End iron works. Along with Proctor and Burton, Richard Duckering and Watkinson and Robey in Lincoln, Marshall's of Gainsborough and Hornsby and Seaman of Grantham the backbone of Lincolnshire's great engineering tradition was established at this time.

Various advertisements appeared in local newspapers concerned with traffic on the river. On 8th September, 1825, one such announced a Methodist missionary meeting in Lincoln, and that Robert Swain, master of a Witham steam packet had been engaged to convey passengers from Boston to the meeting, leaving Boston at 3 o'clock, Dogdyke at 4.30 on 13th September and returning the same evening for a fare of two shillings and sixpence.

An advertisement in the *Stamford Mercury*, of 15th March, 1832, announced:

> The old established Steam Packet Company beg leave most respectfully to return their grateful thanks to the public for all favours conferred on them, and to inform that on Tuesday, the 27th instant, they will commence leaving Boston at 7 o'clock in the morning and arrive at Lincoln in time for coaches to Hull, Leicester, Nottingham and Gainsborough the same day. Best cabin three shillings, second cabin two shillings.

The same newspaper reported, on 13th December, 1827:

> A pleasure boat about 24 feet long, propelled by a small steam engine has recently excited some attention at Boston. The engine is 2¼ horse power, and was constructed by Mr Howden, iron founder. Several partial voyages have been made which completely prove the capability of the engine. On Monday morning the boat started a voyage up the Witham to Lincoln.

An important development took place in 1828 when a Lincoln man, William Poole a whitesmith, invented a new paddle wheel which increased speed by virtue of moving blades which offered less resistance when taking and leaving the water.

The new wheels were fitted to three steam packets, *Favorite*, *Countess of Warwick* and *Witham*, resulting in increased speed and a smaller consumption of fuel.

Trouble appeared from a new source in 1831.

> There seems to be prospects of a tax on passengers using steam packets and it is feared that the fares from Lincoln to Boston will have to be raised to five shillings or more for the best cabin instead of the moderate fares of the day. It is generally expected that the steam boat owners will, if the tax is persisted in, be obliged to dispose of their engines etc. at enormous loss and return to the old usage of towing horses.
>
> There is also a disposition on the part of the Witham Company to cease to allow steam boats in any case as they attribute to them serious injury by washing away the embankments.

Undaunted a speed trial took place on the river in April, between *Favorite* and the *Duchess of St Albans*, the former arriving at Lincoln more than an hour ahead of the 'Duchess'. By June the subject of damage to the river banks was again raised and the question of stopping the steamers renewed.

Accidents were regularly reported. In August 1822, a small boat crewed by man and a boy overturned at Washingborough Ferry whilst trying to land a large hamper of bread from the steam packet. Fortunately the buoyancy of the hamper served as a life preserver until the packet, which had moved off up the river returned and picked up the unfortunate crew. A gentleman on the packet described as Mr Luys, a dancing master, stripped off and went to their assistance. He got the boy on top of the hamper, but owing to the weedy and muddy state of the river could not get them ashore and it was a further twenty minutes or so before the three of them could be extricated from their uncomfortable and perilous situation. On 21st May, 1825, several passengers seated on the upper deck of the *Duke of Sussex*, were thrown below when the seat collapsed. Some were thrown into the river and one was drowned; a verdict of accidental death was recorded at the inquest, 'with a deodand of one shilling upon the packet'.

On 15th November the *Stamford Mercury* recorded as follows:

As the *Victory* Lincoln and Boston steam packet was on her voyage to the latter place on Saturday last, an accident occurred which was attended with serious loss and inconvenience. The man at the helm left his station for a few minutes, a passenger undertaking to steer the packet in his absence. In the interval a Humber keel, laden with corn, which was sailing up the river with a favourable wind blowing very fresh at the time, came in sight suddenly at the turning of the river. The youth, fearful of altering it, allowed it to go on the wrong side, the consequence was that the two vessels came in contact with great violence, the packet having her engine in full play and the corn vessel sailing very fast. The latter struck the packet near the head, tore off the iron railings and part of the deck, and striking the paddle in the centre carried away the greater part of the iron work and bent the shaft, besides otherwise severely damaging the engine.

The packet was crowded with passengers and deeply laden with goods, and the consternation of those on board when the shock first occurred and the vessel nearly turned over cannot be described. The females shrieked and there was a general rush on deck. The scene of ruin which had been accomplished in a moment was suprising to all; the packet which had been pursuing her course so steadily but a moment before lay on the water a shattered hulk, the timbers floating down the river, and the engine stopped. To add to the disaster of the voyage, a dreadful storm of rain and wind prevailed at the time, and it was some hours before horses could be procured to drag the packet to Boston. The *Victory* left Lincoln at 11 o'clock on Saturday morning, and the accident occurred at 2 o'clock in the afternoon, fifteen miles from Boston. Various difficulties presented themselves and upon arriving at Dogdyke, eleven miles from Boston, it was found that the dreadful weather and the heavy load had completely jaded the horses and they were unable to proceed any further.

Another horse was procured after an interval of several hours and the packet finally reached Boston at six o'clock on Sunday morning. It is only an act of justice to Mrs Clayton, the proprietor to say that she did all she could to render the situation as tolerable as possible under the circumstances, and we are sorry to add that she will be a serious sufferer by the accident. The men appear to one and all have deserted the helm on account of the disagreeable weather and left it to the lad.

There were regular boat services along the navigable drains of south Lincolnshire between Boston and the scattered hamlets along the drain banks. In 1856 there were 14 market packet boats which converged on Bargate bridge every Wednesday and Saturday from as far away as Revesby and Hagnaby, and a small craft from Donington and Holland Fen congregated at Black Sluice.

The steam packet traffic reached its zenith during the 1830s, the old wooden hulled vessels being replaced by iron boats of shallower draught and speedier engines. A new company had been formed at Boston to carry cattle to the London markets. Meetings were held to gain the support of the graziers and the Town Clerk of Lincoln was requested to ask the Mayor to call a a public meeting to consider the project. In August 1836 all the shares were taken up and increased in September. In May of the following year the carrying of cattle by boat began, replacing the old system of driving them along roads to London. This naturally enough brought a great deal of protest from the drovers. Depots were established for the convenience of users of the packets, an interesting announcement relating to such a service appearing in October 1836: 'Steam Boat Accommodation. Hannah Clements, Wormgate, Boston, on the death of her husband, intends to carry on the business. Passengers and parcels for the Lincoln Steam and other packets received at her house and goods conveyed to and from the Grand Sluice as usual.'

During the early 1840s the Witham Steam Packet Company operated a daily service between Lincoln and Boston using the packets *Commerce*, *Eclipse*, and *Celerity*. *Ariel* and *Witham* alternately worked a similar service from Slacks warehouse, at Brayford Head. On Fridays steam packets worked to Bardney and Kirkstead, and a horse packet to Horncastle. There was also a daily coach connection to Horncastle from Kirkstead.

Packets worked to Gainsborough four days a week with a Friday service to Saxilby and Torksey. Long distance trade was carried along the Fossdyke to the River Trent, an important link with the Midlands, Humber and Yorkshire. This period just prior to the arrival of the railways in Lincolnshire saw the development of Lincoln and Boston as important trading centres, dealing with the export of farming produce and the import of manufactured goods as well as the more mundane day to day needs of the community.

Trent river traffic in the 1840s, a combination of sail and steam in evidence.

Sir William Cubitt, Engineer to the GNR, who made a considerable impact on the shape of railways in Lincolnshire.

Edmund Denison in 1856. Denison was Chairman of the GNR between 1847 and 1864.

Chapter Three

Early Days, Railway Plans and Schemes

The early history of the Great Northern Railway is a complex web of intrigue and often bitter warfare between rival companies and promoters. There have always been speculators who seek to make money out of the recklessness of investors intent upon gaining high interest on their money. This was certainly the case during the 20 years of railway mania, between 1830 and 1850. This period was interlaced with times of acute depression, hundreds of schemes were put before Parliament, only to be rejected, or to perish after being sanctioned, usually through lack of investment. In Lincolnshire alone there were 84 proposals for railways passing through, or in the vicinity of, the City of Lincoln. The people who benefited most were the professional speculators, lawyers and engineers, rather than the genuine investor. The whole period was a discredit to a large number of people; it does appear, however, that those involved in carrying through the GNR scheme came through it with more credit than most.

As early as 1827, a line going up the valleys of the Lea, Rib, and Quin to Cambridge, and from there to Lincoln, was surveyed by Sir John Rennie, but abandoned. Rennie's scheme was revived in the (1844) Direct Northern Railway proposals.

In 1833, a railway was projected and surveyed by Nicholas Wiles Cundy, which was to run from London, via Bishop's Stortford, Cambridge, Lincoln, Gainsborough and Selby to York, and was to be known as the Grand Northern Railway.

In 1834, James Walker was employed to survey a railway called the Northern and Eastern Railway, running from London to York, via Cambridge and Lincoln with a branch to Norwich. This railway received its Act in 1836. By this time however it had been reduced to a line between London and Cambridge, duplicating Cundy's Grand Northern route to Cambridge. The company joined the Eastern Counties Railway, which completed the line through to Cambridge and Brandon in 1845. By this time proposals were in hand to extend the route north towards York. The Eastern Counties Railway had been sanctioned by an Act of 1836 providing a connection between London, Colchester, Yarmouth and Norwich.

In 1835, Joseph Gibbs proposed a line from Whitechapel via Dunmow, Cambridge, Sleaford to Lincoln and York. To this line was provisionally given the title Great Northern Railway, the first time the name had appeared. The company failed to proceed and the name was not to reappear until it was adopted by the London and York grouping in 1846.

At this time George Stephenson was surveying a line to run from Birmingham to Derby and from there to Leeds, whilst Vignoles was occupied with similar work on a proposal to join the Midland Counties system with that of the London & Birmingham at Rugby.

A York linen draper, George Hudson, was interesting himself in a proposal known as the York and West Riding Railway, its aim to connect York with lines already constructed through which communication with London and the south could be effected. The project was abandoned and the York Corporation Railway Committee began discussing the relative merits of the Northern and Eastern and the Great Northern schemes. In the meantime Hudson had been in touch with Stephenson and, as a result, advocated to the York Committee the construction of a railway from York, to join Stephenson's Derby and Leeds line, known as the North Midland, at Normanton. The Committee agreed and the line was built, the first train leaving York for London on 1st July, 1839. The route was via Normanton, Derby and Rugby, with changes at all those places, and involved a distance of 219 miles.

Prior to Hudson's line being completed, the Great North of England scheme, which intended connecting York with Newcastle, was announced. This proposal strengthened Hudson's position, although through lack of funds, it eventually only reached Croft Bridge, on the Stockton & Darlington line.

Hudson's determination to protect his Midland interests was an added potent ingredient in an already complicated situation, rife with protracted arguments and legal rows. Hudson used all manner of means to prevent any interests threatening his own from succeeding. He proposed competing routes, company amalgamations and used alarmist tactics to thwart rival schemes. In the end his own energetic efforts to protect his interests may well have helped to strengthen the resolve of rival factions and indirectly contributed to their eventual success.

There were many people interested in a direct link between London and York. A great deal of influence was being brought to bear by wealthy landowners and important towns in Lincolnshire and south Yorkshire, both, at that time, without a direct north-south connection.

The Wakefield and Lincoln issued its prospectus in February 1844. The scheme found considerable favour in Lincoln, although some saw it as a possible threat to achieving a direct line to London.

The Cambridge and York scheme also appeared in February, 1844. Planned by James Walker, it was, in fact, the extension of the 1836 Northern and Eastern Railway from Cambridge. This line was to run from the Northern and Eastern line, at Cambridge, the northern end running either directly to York, or else making a junction with the North and Midland. The Cambridge and York was joined by the Great Northern Railway, a revived scheme based on Joseph Gibbs earlier proposals; the company never issued a prospectus, joining with the Cambridge and York instead. The reason for this was that the Cambridge and York had modified its scheme, to the extent that it virtually duplicated the Great Northern proposals. James Walker was asked to survey a direct line between London and Peterborough; he proposed a line from near Kings Cross, through Barnet, Hatfield, Biggleswade, St Neots and Huntingdon to Peterborough; at which point it joined the original line through Lincoln to York. The new group announced itself as the London and York Railway, and, on 3rd May, 1844, published its proposals. It had made an approach to the Direct Northern, but the latter preferred to continue to pursue its own aspirations for the time being.

The Wakefield, Lincoln and Boston Railway (formerly the Wakefield and

Lincoln) was surveyed by William Cubitt, who visited Lincolnshire between 4th and 10th April, 1844. His inspection included the banks of the Witham and Fossdyke and on to Saxilby. He reported that the western bank of the Witham was eminently suitable for a single track railway, with passing places at Tattershall Bridge and Bardney Ferry. He also found suitable conditions along the Lincoln-Saxilby section. At Lincoln, Cubitt felt there was plenty of room on the Holmes for an extensive passenger and goods station. His only reservation was of possible public concern caused by crossing the High Street. This scheme turned out to be an important factor in the final shape of railways in Lincolnshire, and a later, modified form, of its proposals was incorporated into the Great Northern Railway system. Cubitt's contribution, along with those of Gibbs and Walker made a significant contribution to the eventual shape of railways in the county.

The Eastern Counties Railway had taken over the assets of the Northern and Eastern Railway in January, 1844, and was promoting a scheme for a route from Cambridge through Lincoln into Yorkshire. The Wakefield, Lincoln and Boston group was approached by the Eastern Counties with a view to forming a connection between Cambridge and Boston, to the advantage of both companies. The negotiations did not work out, and, on 30th April, the Eastern Counties, decided to proceed with its own proposal for a line through Lincoln to Gainsborough and Doncaster.

By the end of May 1844, there were three companies with proposals for linking London with York: the Direct Northern, the Eastern Counties, and the London and York proposing routes by Walker and Gibbs.

It was obvious the London and York had to decide between the two routes. Was it to be Walker's line, known as the 'Fens' line, or Gibbs 'Towns' line, so named because of its proposed passage through Grantham, Newark, Retford and Doncaster. James Walker resigned his post as Engineer to the London and York on 23rd May, 1844 and was replaced by Joseph Locke. Locke's first report, on 22nd August, suggested a route via Grantham and thence between Newark and Lincoln, with junctions to both towns. Beyond here it would continue through Gainsborough to Doncaster with the rest of the route by negotiation. The route from Lincoln northwards was in direct competition with that proposed by the Wakefield, Lincoln and Boston Company. A meeting between Captain Laws of the Wakefield, Lincoln and Boston group, and Edmund Denison of the London and York, brought about the amalgamation of the two groups under the London and York banner, adding a further £500,000 capital to the undertaking.

The resignation of Locke saw the appointment of William Cubitt to the post of Engineer for the London and York, on 23rd September, 1844. His immediate task was how to combine the two proposals currently supported by the London and York group. His solution was as follows:

1. A main line from London to York, using the route proposed by Gibbs, via Grantham, Newark, Retford and Doncaster   186 miles
2. A loop line from Peterborough via Boston and Lincoln, rejoining the main line at Bawtry   86 miles

3. A branch from Bawtry to Sheffield   20¾ miles
4. A branch from Doncaster to Wakefield   20¼ miles
5. Minor branches to Bedford and Stamford

It was decided that the loop line would follow the east bank of the Witham, rather than the west, as proposed by Cubitt's original survey for the Wakefield Lincoln and Boston, and the line would be double throughout. This was no doubt to help allay aggrieved feelings in Lincoln by-passed by the main line. The official name of the line was the 'Lincoln' line although the 'Loop' line became its accepted title. It was some years, however, before the loop was completed because of disputes between a Bawtry or a Doncaster connection with the main line.

The London and York prospectus was issued on 11th June, 1844, before the decisions, just mentioned, had been taken. Apart from the advantages of a direct link between London, York and Edinburgh, the prospectus talked of the rich farmlands of the fens and Lincolnshire now having the advantage of rail services. Cattle could be moved more quickly to market without the weight loss associated with long journeys along roads. Grain, malt and flour could be moved into the industrial areas of Yorkshire and Lancashire, and manufactured goods and coal sent out from those places.

The prospectus anticipated the resulting loss of trade on the Witham and Fossdyke the coming of the railway would precipitate, by announcing a financial agreement with those navigations.

Although by September the structure of the new railway had been resolved, and support gained from all towns along the route, it still had to pass through Parliament. George Hudson was determined this would not happen. With the Midland Railway already under his control he further strengthened his position in 1845, when he became Chairman of the Eastern Counties Railway. This would allow Hudson a base in Cambridge to make a cross-country route joined to the Midland, or a line running north of Cambridge, effectively blocking the east coast route of the London and York. He was extremely energetic in his opposition, proposing alternative schemes, and uniting existing companies through their opposition to the London-York route. He did not succeed, failing to convince promoters that if he was successful in preventing the east coast route he would continue to safeguard his Midland interests.

The London and York proposals were put before Parliament, along with 244 other Railway Bills, in 1845. The Direct Northern and the Cambridge and Lincoln plans were rejected. The London and York fared better, but due to excessive delays, caused mainly by the Hudson group, the Bill, although approved, ran out of time in the House of Lords.

During the next session of Parliament, Hudson changed his tactics, firstly engineering an agreement between the Eastern Counties and the Cambridge and Lincoln group, proposing a line running from Cambridge to Lincoln, Doncaster and York. Secondly, he proposed an Eastern Counties amalgamation with the London and York. The project was carefully considered by the London and York, but confident of its own success, it rejected the offer.

After another attempt to launch its own scheme failed, the Direct Northern amalgamated with the London and York, on 5th May, 1846, the new, enlarged company taking the title Great Northern Railway Company.

Royal Assent was granted on 26th June, 1846. It was in no small part due to Edmund Denison's resolve that the Bill succeeded. His desire to benefit his constituency town of Doncaster was also an important factor in determining the route of the main line to York. The London and York's solicitor, Robert Baxter, dealt with Hudson's wild utterances about engineering difficulties and cost estimates with well-informed, well-reasoned arguments. Joseph Pease, a north country Quaker, supported the London and York's promised through rate for coal traffic, and went as far as offering to guarantee the £300,000, which the promoters had credited themselves for coal traffic.

The Lincolnshire connection on the London and York Board was represented by six Directors. George Hussey Packe, of Claythorpe, was intimately involved with Lincolnshire railways, becoming Chairman of the GNR between 1864 and 1874, having been Vice-Chairman prior to that. Charles Chaplin, of Blankney, with Packe and Denison was also involved with the East Lincolnshire Railway. Other Board members were three county MPs, Trollope, Turner, and Christopher and the Hon. Alexander Leslie-Melville, representing the principal Lincolnshire bankers, Smith, Ellison and Company.

The line at Spalding, October 1848.

Grand Sluice, Boston

A postcard view of Grand Sluice railway bridge at Boston.

The railway companies represented in this photograph of Lincoln include the GNR, who built the station, the Great Central, who built the class '11' 4-4-0 No. 694, and the Great Eastern, whose wooden office stands on the platform above the engine's front buffer beam. The date is 12th August, 1899, No. 694 seen here in rebuilt form, was one of a class of only six engines based on a Parker design but built by Pollitt.

LCGB/Ken Nunn Collection

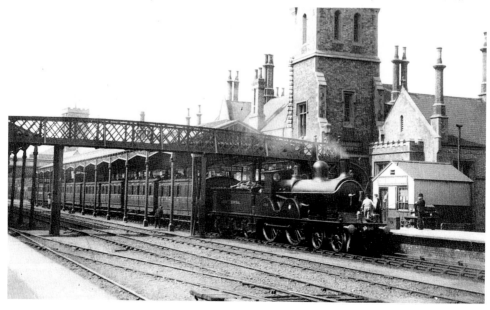

Chapter Four

Railways Arrive in Lincolnshire

At the first meeting of the GNR, held at 36, Great George Street, Westminster, on 1st July, 1846, William Anstell, MP was appointed Chairman, Edmund Denison and Samuel James Capper were made Deputy Chairmen. William Cubitt was Consulting Engineer, his son Joseph to be the Engineer for the southern part of the line and Mr Miller for the northern section. Three assistant Engineers were appointed for the loop line, George Sherrard, at Tattershall, Mr Bryden, at Spalding and Mr Brockedon, at Lincoln. A committee was set up to manage the Foss and Witham navigations, with Thomas Keyworth as canal manager.

By the middle of August important decisions had been taken regarding the construction of the railway. The 20 miles, or so, north of London were to be the heaviest in terms of cost and construction. Problems were also anticipated crossing the fens in Huntingdon. The decision was taken to give priority to the construction of the Lincolnshire Loop line, which would be relatively straightforward from an engineering point of view and put the company where it could earn some much needed revenue fairly quickly. It was estimated the line would take about 14 months to complete.

In November 1846, Thomas Brassey agreed to construct the main line between Kings Cross and Peterborough and Samuel Morton Peto and Edward Ladd Betts agreed to complete the Loop line by 28th February, 1848. The contract was based on a schedule of prices and later, in October 1847, included the construction of stations and other buildings. It also carried a penalty clause of £1,000 a week. Peto and Betts established offices in a large house, to the west of the river in Boston, in March 1847. The GNR had Parliamentary sanction to continue the Lincoln line north of Gainsborough to rejoin the main line at Bawtry, at which point access was to be gained to the Sheffield branch. However, the Parliamentary Committee of 1845 rejected the idea of the branch, thus removing the need for a Bawtry connection. William Cubitt suggested continuing the line northwards to join the main line at Rossington. A Deviation Bill was presented to Parliament, the GNR feeling that all sections of the Loop line would be open by early 1848, allowing travel from Peterborough, through Boston and Lincoln to York. The company's confidence was, however, misplaced; the Bill was rejected by Parliamentary Committee, because of strong objections registered by landowners. The Loop remained incomplete until 1867.

Advertisements were placed for supplies for rails and sleepers specifying wrought iron reversible rails, weighing 72 lb. to the yard. The sleepers, of Memel Fir, were to be triangular, four cut from balks 1 ft 1 in. square by 8 ft 6 in. long. The tender price was to include delivery to the ports of Boston, Spalding, Gainsborough, Goole, Wisbech, Lynn and London.

A foundry, standing on land purchased by the GNR near Durham Ox Inn in Lincoln, was used to cast iron chairs to a design patented to Ransomes and May, pig iron being shipped in through Boston for the purpose. Production, under the direction of Benjamin Cubitt, began in December 1846, the foundry soon producing enough chairs weekly to lay one mile of railway. (The foundry was later used as temporary workshops prior to the opening of Boston Works.) A large ballast field was established near Hartsholme, and work started on Sincil Dyke bridge, near Lincoln Station, a diversion of the dyke required at this point. By October 1847, the work was almost completed. Progress was also being made on the Lincoln to Gainsborough section, work concentrating on the large cuttings beyond Saxilby.

Miller resigned as Engineer for the northern section and was replaced by Joseph Cubitt, who assumed the rôle of Superintending Engineer for the whole system, responsible to his father.

On 5th February, Joseph Cubitt was able to report that the permanent way between Peterborough and Spalding had been ballasted for a distance of about eight miles, and that every effort was being made to have as much permanent way as possible laid in advance, so that ballasting could go ahead without interruption. Between Boston and Lincoln, 13 miles of track had been ballasted, and it was anticipated that the line between Peterborough and Gainsborough would be open by September, that year.

It is well to remember that these railways were made by pick and shovel method, with very little mechanical assistance. This required a considerable workforce. The skilled labouring jobs would fall to experienced navvies, who moved from job to job, often following a particular employer. Much of the rest of the workforce would be recruited locally. As the Lincolnshire lines were relatively easy to construct, it is likely that much of the labour was recruited locally. Working for the railway would have offered a higher wage than agricultural work, except during harvest time. It was noted that progress on the construction of the Loop line slowed considerably during the months of July and August, 1847, as large numbers of workers returned to the land for the harvest, coming back to the railway in September.

Most of the money earned by the navvies was spent on food and drink. The local newspapers complained of intemperance and uproar night after night caused by navvies and local troublemakers: '. . . . local inhabitants living in a state of constant terror'. Navvies left behind bills unpaid to tradepeople who allowed credit, or those who let lodgings, in some cases the losses were severe. They also took local women with them, in some cases, 'the wives of decent men and mothers of families, who had been induced to rob their husbands and abscond'.

On many occasions, however, it was the navvies who were the recipients of injustice. A good example is the case of sub-contractor Wolds, who, in December 1847, made off with the wages of fourteen navvies. They followed him as far as the Witham Tavern and took him outside to settle the matter, whereupon they were set upon by about 30 men who gave them a severe beating.

In March 1848, a total of 1,424 men and 76 horses were working on the Boston section of the line. Generally the men were well behaved, the *Stamford Mercury* reporting that the May Fair had been the most trouble free for a good many years. One cause of the navvies' good behaviour was thought to be because the contractors would not pay the men's wages in public houses.

On the credit side, local people gained by the presence of the railway and its workers, from the sale of timber, food and beer. Iron had to be imported, but bricks could be made locally; Deeping St James, was such a place on the Loop line. Many small firms benefited by the demand for railway equipment, for example, Smith's timber yard at Gainsborough installed a steam operated saw bench to meet the railway's demands for timber.

It is ironic that the river trade through the port of Gainsborough boomed for a short period after 1837, when stone, lime and timber was required for the construction of railway stations, tunnels, bridges. However, after 1851 trade at the port declined, the railway being regarded as the main culprit.

At a GNR Board meeting on 25th February, 1848, William Cubitt, Edward Bury, the newly appointed locomotive engineer, and Captain Laws, were requested to estimate the number of engines and carriages required for the opening of the Loop line. The Cubitts were also instructed to proceed with the construction of workshops at Boston, and to remove all tools from the Lincoln Foundry, which was to be demolished.

At Peterborough it was decided to use the Eastern Counties station as a temporary terminus for the Loop line trains, until a GNR station was built. Access would be over the Midland Railway by a connection at Walton Junction. Agreement with the Midland was achieved at Derby on 6th September, 1848, the GNR agreeing to pay 66 per cent of the receipts as a maximum toll. The cost of using the Eastern Counties station was eventually settled by arbitration.

The GNR station at Peterborough and the hotel and engine shed, were all designed by the Lincoln architect, Henry Goddard, and all the buildings were erected by the contracting firm of F.W. Costar.

By July 1848, Cubitt reported that 50 miles of permanent way had been laid on the Loop line, 42½ miles of it double track.

With the completion of the workshop buildings at Boston, Bury was authorised to install machinery and fittings. He made the most of the opportunity by persuading the GNR Directors of the difficulties involved in obtaining the machinery and then, having been given a free hand, proceeded to use his own firm, Bury, Curtis, and Kennedy, as supplier. Bury was also charged with the task of determining the number, and grades, of various officers required to operate the line and their rates of pay. Those who were to be clothed and lodged by the company had to be identified and instructions to be issued to employees in the locomotive and the carriage departments formulated. It was his job also to present a list of stores required for the opening of the line, and to suggest how they might be obtained. Bury was further involved, along with Captain Laws and the Cubitts, in devising a signalling system. These four gentlemen plus Baxter were to prepare a draft of the Bye Laws, to be exhibited at stations for the guidance of the public. Although work on the Loop progressed well to the north and south of Boston, several factors caused delays to work in the town itself. Early problems were caused by the crossing of West Street at its junction with Butts Lane. The East Lincolnshire Railway intended crossing West Street at the George Street junction, in order to reach its proposed Pulvertoft Lane terminus. Eventually both companies agreed to form a common line into Boston; crossing West Street at the Bond Street junction, this would have necessitated crossing the Witham south of the Grand Sluice. However, Admiralty surveyors refused permission for a bridge south of the Grand Sluice and, despite an appeal by the East Lincolnshire Railway, and a public hearing in Boston on 25th May, 1847, the decision stood. Both companies were obliged to cross West Street, west of the Queen Street Junction.

Work did not begin in Boston until 9th October, 1847, when the first piles were driven into the Witham for the Grand Sluice bridge. By January 1848, all piles had been driven, all the lower walling capsills completed and almost all the corbels were in position. The structure of the bridge was completed in February, although it did not open to traffic immediately. In the meantime the railway was approaching Boston along the banks of the Witham; on 10th March, GNR No. 2, a 'little Sharpie' locomotive on loan to Peto and Betts, brought 72 ballast wagons up to Howden's Phoenix Ironworks, on the east side of the Witham, alongside the Grand Sluice. During the spring between six and eight ballast trains worked between the ballast pits at Tattershall and Boston, the journey taking about 90 minutes.

The GNR found local landowners in Boston asking exhorbitant prices for land required by the railway company. William Howden, the owner of the Phoenix Ironworks, demanded £10,000 for land valued at little more than £100. Councillor Holliday William Hartley, who lived at Witham Bank East, asked £2,700 for an acre of his land. He arrived home on 19th January, 1848, to find a substantial fence erected along the river bank, within yards of his, and his neighbours', front doors, destroying shrubs and lawns. This bold move by the GNR, fearful of delays in opening the line, certainly got building underway in Boston, but resulted in an acrimonious court case. Brought by Hartley and Thomas Hopkins, the case was heard at Lincoln Assizes in 1849. The ruling of the court was that the GNR should pay compensation to the injured parties as well as paying the cost of the case.

The opening of the Grand Sluice Bridge took place on the damp drizzly evening of 25th May, the *Boston Herald* describing the scene as follows:

At about quarter of a mile from the old brewery on the west bank, the powerful six-wheel engine, No. 2, was stationed, puffing and snorting like an eager racer waiting for the signal to start. At 8 o'clock, the line was cleared and shortly afterwards the steam was put on, the shrill whistle sounded and the iron horse approached the bridge at a steady pace, propelling about 25 heavily laden ballast wagons in advance. The wagons proceeded slowly across the newly-constructed line for a couple of hundred yards, when it was found that the impetus was not sufficient to propel so heavy a train over the curve, which is rather acute (the radius being 8 chains). The train was accordingly backed for a few hundred yards, additional impetus given, and at exactly 25 minutes past 9, the train proceeded majestically and safely across the bridge.

Although the opening of the Lincolnshire Loop line was preceded by that of the East Lincolnshire Railway, on 2nd October, celebrations were reserved for the opening of the Loop. The line opened on 17th October, and was followed on 26th by a 'Great Railway Holiday', in Boston, celebrating the, 'annihilation of time and space' by rail travel.

The original venue for a dinner to be held in the evening, was to have been the Guildhall, but due to the demand for tickets the Guildhall's capacity was too limited, and the event was moved to the Red Lion Theatre. The orchestra pit was boarded over and 400 people sat down for a meal provided by Daniel Jackson, of the Peacock Hotel. The distinguished guests included John Noble, the Mayor of Boston, Samuel Morton Peto, the Earl of Yarborough, Edmund Denison, George Hussey Packe and the town's two MPs, Sir James Duke and Benjamin Bond Cabell. A ball was later held in the Assembly Rooms.

This event had been preceded by a tea party for 600 working men and their families, which took place in the Town Hall during the afternoon.

The *Illustrated London News*, described the day's events:

Opening of the Great Northern Railway

On the 17th inst the Loop Line of the Great Northern Railway communication in Lincolnshire was opened with great éclat. Two well-filled trains left Peterborough at 6 am and 9 am and were hailed along the line by crowds who flocked to see them pass. At twelve o'clock a train with passengers from the London North Western and the Eastern Counties followed. Among those connected with the undertaking were Mr James Arboin, Mr Pym, Mr Mowatt, Mr Cubitt, the engineer, Mr Scott Russell, Mr Bury, the locomotive superintendent, Mr Pulford, his manager, Mr Williams, and others. The train arrived at Boston about two, at Lincoln soon after three and was greeted between Boston and Lincoln with bands of music and masses of people.

The entire line lies on a dead level; and the only difficulty has been in securing a firm foundation in some parts of the fens. The stations are plain and inexpensive and the whole line has been constructed at £15,000 per mile, or a total of one million for the 64 miles. It consists of that portion of the Great Northern Railway known as the 'loop line', from its coiling round in that form from the main point at Peterborough, and embracing within its circuit of 64 miles, Spalding, Boston, Lincoln and the adjacent districts; carrying traffic southward on the one hand, by means of the London North Western Railway, and on the other by means of the Eastern Counties, both of which have a terminal extension at Peterborough. This, however, is a temporary arrangement for working the Lincolnshire traffic over the 'Loop' until the main line of the Great Northern, on their arrival at Boston, will unite with those of the East Lincolnshire Railway, now completed to the latter point; and will be taken by that railway on to Louth and Grimsby, and the passenger steamers over the Humber to Hull; the great advantage being that passengers and goods may be conveyed direct without interruption, to and from London to Hull, by way of Peterborough, 40 miles shorter than by any other route, and at a saving of two hours.

The distance from Peterborough to Boston is 32 miles, and from Boston to Lincoln 30. The chief peculiarity in the structure of the line is that all the bridges are built of timber. The line from Peterborough to Boston is, 16 miles continuously straight, besides being level, or pretty nearly so. It is provided at all stations with cattle pens for agricultural purposes. The steepest gradient is 1 in 100. The contractors have been Mr Peto and Mr Betts.

In December 1848, the Lincolnshire Committee of the GNR reported its dissatisfaction with some of the work carried out by the Cubitts and the contractor Peto. The layout of Lincoln station, carriage shed and gatekeepers' lodges, was considered unsatisfactory. The only permanent building

'270' series 0-4-2WT No. 270A at Lincoln on 4th August, 1902. Built by Neilson in 1867 No. 270A is seen here in her final form. *LCGB/Ken Nunn Collection*

GNR '229' class 2-2-2 No. 240 at Lincoln where it worked as carriage pilot. Seen here with a Stirling tender in 1897. *LCGB/Ken Nunn Collection*

completed at Boston was the carriage shed, although work was in progress on the workshops and engine shed. Water cranes at Lincoln and Boston were situated such that engines had to be detached from their trains to take water. Peto was paying three men two shillings and sixpence a day to pump water at Boston, but charging the company three shillings and sixpence.

It had taken the GNR until June 1848, to purchase sufficient land just north of the West Street crossing at Boston to allow work to begin on a temporary station. This had two 500 ft long platforms and very modest buildings, the only permanent ones being the large carriage shed and a water tank. The permanent station, designed by Henry Goddard, was sited a little to the east of the temporary one and opened in November 1850. It had distinctive iron canopies which enclosed the platform lines and a new refreshment room was included. In 1864 a covered footbridge was erected together with new waiting rooms. In 1911, the original 1848 five-arch entrance was abandoned in favour of a new entrance to the south, the works also including a central booking office and covered access to the footbridge. New waiting rooms were added and the parcels office moved to the old entrance which had two of its arches demolished.

The GNR station at Lincoln was the second station opened in the City, the first being the Midland station, completed during 1846. Lincoln Great Northern was designed by the London architect, John Taylor. Built by Peto and Betts, using grey bricks to a mock-Tudor design, the station was dominated by a tower, part of the main building on the north platform. Originally the station comprised two main through lines, two platforms on loops as well as small goods and coal facilities. Powers to extend the station area were obtained on 1st August, 1849, and this was an ongoing process for a good many years. The original crossing gates in the High Street were the shorter overlapping type, operated manually by a gateman. When the gates were installed the intention was that they would close off roadway, leaving the railway lines open. This was because of the lack of road traffic at this time. At some point it was decided to reverse this situation thus leaving the gates open to road traffic. It appears this decision was made by local railway authority, no doubt under pressure from the local authority, claiming that the passage of pedestrians was restricted by the gates closed over the roadway. A footbridge was built at the crossing in 1874 and lasted until 1991 when crossing gates were replaced by lifting barriers.

Originally there was no signal box at the crossing but one was installed in the early 1850s, replacing the rectory of the church of St Mary-le-Wigford, which had previously occupied the site. Signalling at the station was updated by Saxby and Farmer in 1882.

It is thought that the first entrance to the station off the High Street, was via Wigford Place. A new entrance was made from St Mary Street in 1882.

An early map of the station, dated 1851, shows the position of the signal box, although whether it was built at this time is unclear. A substantial building, to the south of the southern platform, was the goods shed which was eventually used for the storage of private carriages. Plans exist showing a row of wagon turntables at the west end of the building but these were never installed. The building was removed in the 1882 proposals for increased accommodation. A second down platform and extension of the Boston end of the up platform with double and single line bays were included in these proposals. In 1884 canopies were erected over the platform tracks.

Prior to this on the Holmes, an engine shed, a new goods shed and yard extensions were completed by October 1876.

In its final form the station had six through roads, including two centre ones often used for carriage storage or for running round. There were three through platforms and four bays let into the eastern end of the north side. The main platforms were Nos. 5 and 6 with No. 7 on the outer face of the island platform, and side platform No. 8. The bays were numbered 1 to 4.

The track arrangements at Lincoln were extremely complex. There were huge yards on either side especially at the west end where were located the 'Bog' sidings. Goods shed, cattle and coal depots were all on the north side with a fan shape of five sidings for each direction on the south side backed by the engine shed, with its 70 ft turntable and coaling plant. Further south were more sidings whose outlets faced west. From High Street level crossing and the swing bridge over Brayford Pool the running lines fanned out from East Holmes signal box to come together again at West Holmes. Here a reverse loop went to Boultham Junction on the avoiding line.

Pelham Street Junction at the east end of the station had a busy time by virtue of its level crossing and lines running off in four directions to Barnetby, Boston, Sleaford, and a further reversing loop to the avoiding line.

On 6th June, 1883, a short spur of one mile in length chiefly on a viaduct was opened by the GNR from Washingborough Junction to Greetwell East Junction. Constructed by Baker and Firbank, this enabled GNR goods workings to avoid Lincoln station by use of the avoiding line which opened in August 1882. At the western end of the line a short spur ran from Boultham Junction round to West Holmes Junction to enable GNR goods traffic to reach the yards without fouling the station area and its crossings.

Train tickets were collected at the previous stopping station for trains approaching from the east, an incoming ticket platform on the Holmes dealt with trains from the north and west.

The GNR station served several other companies. The Manchester, Sheffield and Lincolnshire Railway had running powers for all traffic between Sykes Junction and Lincoln, as well as entry over Pelham Street Junction for the north-east. The MS&LR's future partner, in what became the Great Central Railway, the Lancashire, Derbyshire and East Coast Railway, also ran into the GNR station. The Great Eastern Railway obtained powers to run passengers trains from Sincil Junction to Pyewipe Junction, completing its passenger route to Yorkshire, in conjunction with the Great Northern and Great Eastern Joint Railway.

The North Eastern Railway worked the York trains prior to the 1923 Grouping. The Lancashire and Yorkshire Railway only used its running powers for race excursions.

There were no distinct company allocations in the station, the use of the platforms being governed by convenience. With the growth of traffic, and before the construction of the bay platforms on the north side, the centre island platform was often worked in both directions.

The GNR built the Great Northern Hotel next to High Street crossing. In keeping with the old Inn tradition, within which most establishments incorporated the name of the owner or tenant in the inn sign, the Great Northern Hotel was originally known as as 'Moyes Great Northern Hotel and Posting House'. The tenants name, Moyes appearing on the nameboard at the highest point over the entrance archway. Mr Moyes turned out to be an unsatisfactory tenant, leaving the hotel in 1853, owing the GNR nearly £900, most of which was written off as a bad debt. After this time the hotel became known as the Great Northern Hotel.

A good view of Lincoln Central station as it appeared in the early 1900s.
Peter Grey Collection

A 1905 view of the ferry at Langrick showing two interesting pleasure boats. Compare this view with the one below, taken from the same spot. *D.N. Robinson Collection*

The ferry at Langrick was replaced by a girder bridge in 1907. The postcard dated 8th August, reads, 'The bridge is close by our house and is just being finished. The river runs by our garden gate and we sit on the bank for hours watching steamers and skiffs come up the river.' *D.N. Robinson Collection*

Chapter Five

The GNR and the River Witham

The opening of the railways in Lincolnshire offered a quicker, more reliable and comfortable passenger service than those offered by coach or waterways, as well as providing a faster means of transporting greater quantities of goods. Some waterways lost all their traffic within 30 years of the appearance of the railways, others were still in commercial use after World War I.

Stations were located close to the main river-packet landing places, thus creating direct competition between boats and trains. Cattle pens, provided at many stations, facilitated the transportation of livestock throughout the country, and as a result, the takings at toll gates on roads, by which livestock had previously been moved, fell dramatically. Stage coaches were reduced to the status of feeder services to the rail network.

Passenger traffic did continue on the Witham, despite the introduction of Parliamentary trains offering facilities for third class passengers. In 1850 the GNR offered fourth class travel between Boston and Lincoln, at a fare of 1s. 3d. By 1863 the packet boats were finished, although freight continued to be moved by water, albeit to a much lesser degree. The amount of coal passing through the Grand Sluice in 1847 was 19, 535 tons, this fell to 3,780 tons by 1854. Total tonnage for the Witham fell from 276,154 tons in 1848, to to 18,548, in 1904.

Market boats on the navigable drains north and west of Boston were not in direct competition with the railways and continued to sail into the town until replaced by motor buses in the early 1920s.

The GNR directly leased the Witham and Fossdyke navigations, and despite neglect, they survived longer than their independent counterparts. The Witham was governed by seven authorities:

1. The Witham Outfall Board, who maintained the bed of the river from the outfall of the new cut to the Grand Sluice, and the banks between the outfall and Hobhole Sluice.
2. The Boston Court of Sewers, who maintained the banks from Hobhole to the Grand Sluice.
3. The Boston Harbour Commissioners, who were responsible for controlling navigation over the same stretch of river.
4. The Lincoln Court of Sewers was similarly responsible for the bed and banks from Brayford Mere up to Stapleford Bridge, about 20 miles north of Grantham.
5. The Grantham Court of Sewers was similarly responsible for Stapleford Bridge up to the source of the river.
6. The Witham General Commissioners, whose responsibility was the bed between Grand Sluice and Bardney Lock, as well as the west bank of that length.
7. The GNR Company, who maintained the east bank of the same length, the Witham General Commissioners paying the company £2,800 per annum for repairing the east bank.

In 1846 the railway company took over the rights and liabilities of the company of Proprietors of the Witham Navigation, under a lease of 999

Bardney Bridge, *c.* 1916, The old flat bed ferry, which the bridge replaces, is seen on the opposite side of the River Witham. *D.N. Robinson Collection*

A view similar in location to the engraving which appears as the front endpaper. This photograph was taken in the early part of the twentieth century and shows the heavily populated Stamp End area of Lincoln with Stamp End lock in the foreground.

Author's Collection

The ferry across the Fossdyke near Rolands Siding, off Ferry Lane, Skellingthorpe, in 1932.

years. They maintained Bardney Lock and Stamp End Lock, in Lincoln; the
bed of the river from Bardney Lock to Brayford Mere, the Sincil Dyke and
the Bargate Weir and Sluices; the bank of the old river at Branston Island,
and both banks above Bardney Lock, except those bordering the
Washingborough and Heighington Drainage District Board, to whom the
company paid £2,000 to discharge that part of their liability.

The areas which suffered most flooding in very wet seasons were the low
parts of Lincoln and the low land in the West Lincoln Drainage area, above
Lincoln up to the River Till.

Bardney Lock was located 22½ miles above Grand Sluice and Stamp End Lock
about 30½ miles above the same point. At Stamp End Lock there was a weir and
sluices, and higher up the river, above Lincoln, the Bargate Weir and Sluices at
the head of Sincil Dyke. The object of these weirs was to hold up the water for
the navigation of the Witham and the Fossdyke.

Under the Act of 1812 the Company of Proprietors of the Witham Navigation
were directed to erect a good substantial lock, with a stone weir or outfall, and
with sluices of sufficient capacity for the passage for the flood waters at, or near,
Stamp End Lock. Increased passage for the flood waters was to be made by the
construction of a weir and sluices in the east bank of the river at the head of
Bargate Drain. In pursuance of the Act two civil engineers, John Farnworth, of
Boston, and George Leather, of Leeds, in an award dated 8th September, 1831,
fixed levels for the weirs as prescribed by the Act.

The GNR fixed a nine inch board on top of Stamp Weir and sluices, ostensibly
to maintain an adequate depth of water for navigation, however, a report by
Richard Grantham and Charles Bidwell in 1915 suggested that the GNR had
fixed the board in place to spare themselves the expense of dredging the river,
and also expressed some doubt as to whether the company was legally entitled
to raise the discharge level of the weir above the statutory level, especially
having regard to the added danger of flooding of the low-lying parts of the City
of Lincoln and the lands above the City:

> When we saw the board it was holding the water at a level of about four inches above
> the top of the weir. At ordinary times no harm may be done, but in flood times, when
> the water rises to the top of the board, and it is not allowed to escape by the drawing of
> the sluices until it reaches a level of nine inches above the top of the weir is very
> manifest.

Mr Mudford, solicitor for the GNR, stated that the board had been in place at
the weir for very many years and that it was there 'under authority'; he made
assurances that the GNR would continue to maintain it.

Chapter Six

The Route Described

The Lincolnshire Loop ran through interminably flat countryside and apart from a hump near Peakirk, gradients were slight. From Werrington Junction, north of Peterborough, to Boston the railway ran in a north-north-easterly direction, along what was probably the longest stretch of straight level track to be found in the United Kingdom. Its course beyond Boston was very different, mostly following the curves of the River Witham to Lincoln. It was always said that when they built the Loop the GNR had a lot of rails to spare so they decided to use them all! This is a reference to the circuitous nature of the Boston-Lincoln section.

There were 42 level crossings and six road bridges, one over the line, the rest under, between Peterborough and Lincoln. The many watercourses required the construction of 32 viaducts, seven with cast iron girders, the rest of timber. The most notable were at Bardney and Boston. At the latter the structure consisted of short spans supported on massive piles driven into the river bed. Near Bardney the railway crossed the Witham at Horsley Deeps, by means of a structure which required a centre span long enough to allow navigation of the river. A total length of 729 yards, the main girders consisted of huge timber arches, from which the rail carrying deck was suspended, an elegant structure using some £30,000 worth of timber in its construction. There is a beautiful scale model of the Bardney viaduct in the National Railway Museum, York. After fire destroyed a wooden bridge near Deeping Fen in July 1849, the GNR Directors became apprehensive about other wooden bridges on the system and resolved to build a cottage for the bridge keeper at Brayford Mere swivel bridge, and keep a fire engine at Bardney bridge.

In July 1858 it was decided to replace the Bardney structure, which would appear to be a poor return for the original outlay of its construction. Walter Brydone, the GNR Engineer at that time, decided to divert along a 1,440 embankment, making the length of the new bridge 745 ft, with two spans of 60 ft and one of 90 ft, with fixed girders, resting on cylinders sunk into the riverbed, the shorter spans on brickwork. The reconstruction was carried out by F. Rummens, using plate girders made by Butler and Co. of Stanningley, the work being completed at the end of 1860. Sincil Dyke bridge was also rebuilt soon after this time.

The bridge at Boston fared a little better surviving until 1885, when it was replaced by a new three span plate and box girder structure, designed by Richard Johnson, the GNR's Chief Engineer, and constructed by Matthew Pitts. The new bridge was tested by six engines running over it prior to its opening on 20th May. At the same time Maud Foster Drain bridge, of wooden construction, was replaced by an iron structure, at a cost of £805.

The line was double except for a quarter mile at the junction at Boston. The GNR obtained an Act of 1st August, 1849 for a deviation at Boston, which sanctioned the enlargement of the stations there and at Lincoln. Charles Ward,

Class 'B1' 4-6-0 No. 61073 with the 3 pm, Boston train, leaving Peterborough North on 16th August, 1958.   *P.H. Groom*

A busy scene at the north end of Peterborough North, class 'C12' 4-4-2T No. 67938, class 'N5' 0-6-2T No. 69293, class 'V2' 2-6-2 No. 60908 and Immingham based class 'B1' 4-6-0 No. 61130 creating plenty of steam and smoke in 1957.   *Andrew C. Ingram Collection*

Class 'J6' 0-6-0 No. 64192 arrives at Peterborough North with a local train in 1958.
Andrew C. Ingram Collection

LNER class 'C12' 4-4-2T No. 67376 shunting past North box at Peterborough, 1957.
A.V. Fincham

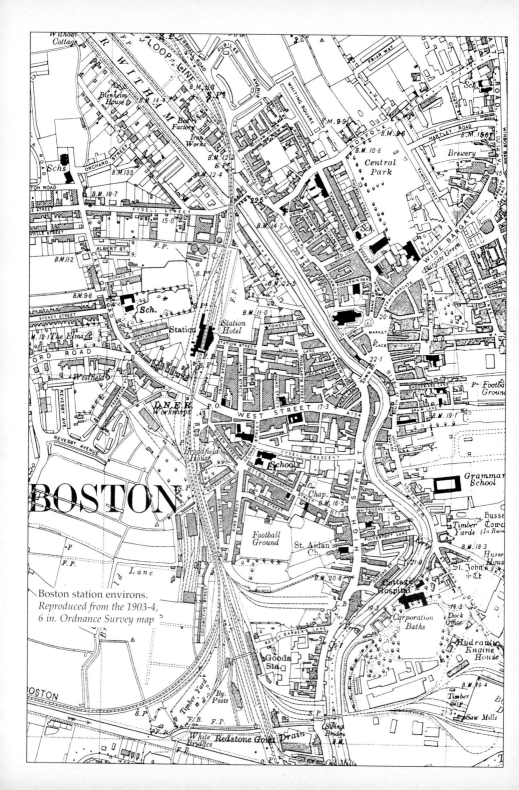

BOSTON

Boston station environs.
*Reproduced from the 1903-4,
6 in. Ordnance Survey map*

Rebuilt GNR 2-2-2 No. 232 at East Lincoln Junction, Boston on 13th August, 1907.

Pilcher Collection, NRM

GNR superheated class 'J21' 0-6-0 No. 74 with a Kings Cross-Skegness Bank Holiday excursion passing East Lincoln box, at Boston on 4th August, 1913. *Pilcher Collection, NRM*

A view of Boston station in the 1960s with the platform roofs and the centre through roads still *in situ*.   *Douglas Thompson*

A general view of Boston station in April 1968 the earlier platform roofs having been replaced by nasty little awnings.   *Andrew C. Ingram Collection*

A class 'B17' 4-6-0 No. 61643 *Champion Lodge* crosses Grand Sluice Bridge, Boston with the 9.07 am Doncaster to March, in June 1958.   *Les Perrin*

Immingham based class 'K3' 2-6-0 No. 61800 with a freight train at Sleaford Junction, Boston on 23rd June 1958. This train terminated at Boston and the locomotive went on shed.   *R.C. Riley*

of Lincoln, constructed the deviation at Boston, which included 52 chains of railway, 13 chains of which were on the East Lincolnshire line. He completed the work and it was connected up to the old lines on Sunday 11th May, 1850, thus making the Loop double throughout.

Intermediate stations on the line were at Peakirk, Littleworth, Spalding and Algarkirk, between Peterborough and Boston, then Langrick, Tattershall, Kirkstead, Stixwould, Southrey, Bardney, Five Mile House and Washingborough to Lincoln. Nearly all the Boston to Lincoln stations were adjacent to ferries across the Witham. Although Kirton and Surfleet were constructed for the opening of the line they were not opened until 3rd April, 1849. It was also decided at this time to construct a passenger platform, siding and wharf at Dogdyke, on the Witham. These works were carried out by Stephen Dawson, and opened in 1849. Boston works charged five shillings for fixing the nameboards. Eight shillings was the charge for making nameboards for 'Crowland', which opened on the Peterborough to Boston stretch, on 1st August, 1849. This station eventually settled for the name, 'St James Deeping'. Five Mile House station was closed on 2nd December, 1850, after average weekly receipts of only nine shillings and fourpence were reported to the GNR Board. In 1865 an important farmer in the district requested a private siding at the station. This was duly installed and the station reopened, possibly in August of that year.

In 1848, the GNR had reached as far as Lincoln and work was progressing on the 15½ miles between the City and Gainsborough; by the end of the year the Loop line had reached Saxilby and the bridge over the Fossdyke there had been completed.

On 15th March, 1849, Henry Fowler was appointed Resident Engineer for the lines from Peterborough to Gainsborough and from Boston to Grimsby. On 29th March, the Lincoln to Gainsborough section was inspected by Captain Wynne, who insisted on the erection of signals at the swing bridge at Brayford Mere, before the line could open. Captain Wynne was also surprised to discover the junction with the MS&LR at Gainsborough which was not authorised. The GNR stated that the Acts of both companies, allowed their lines to cross on the level and the junction was merely a curve, allowed under General Powers, and also that it would be inconvenient not to have the junction. The line between Lincoln and Gainsborough opened on Easter Monday, 9th April, 1849.

Leaving Lincoln station the line crossed High Street on the level, continued over the Witham by a drawbridge, and along the south bank of the Fossdyke as far as Saxilby, where it crossed the navigation. This section was on the level, but beyond here, to Gainsborough, there were some earthworks, sharp gradients and bridges. Stations were at Saxilby and Marton. Although work had begun on the station at Lea, work had been brought to a standstill on the instructions of the GNR Board and the station did not open until 1st August.

Gainsborough Junction faced Retford and necessitated the reversal of GNR trains to gain access to the MS&LR station. By an agreement of 1st June, 1848, use of the station was to be paid for all classes of traffic equal to two miles of the maximum MS&LR charges.

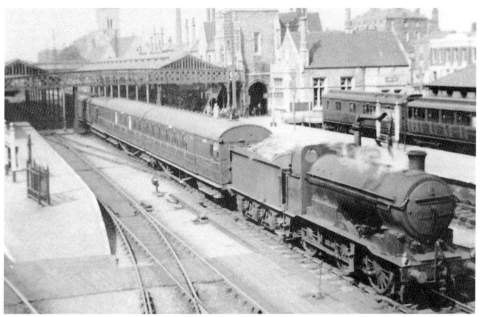

0-6-0 No. 3600 on a Boston train standing on the down through line at Lincoln station before backing into the up bay platform, 10th September, 1937.   *Charles Bayes*

An overall view of Lincoln Central station with the church of St Mary-le-Wigford just beyond, this view taken on 3rd May, 1975.   *N.D. Mundy*

LNER 'C12' 4-4-2T No. 4009A stands at platform 4 on station pilot duties at Lincoln Central on 10th May, 1946. *H.C. Casserley*

Ex-GNR '854' series, No. 3908 brings a freight train through Lincoln Central station and across High Street crossing on 8th June, 1926. *H.C. Casserley*

Lincoln, showing the converging railways. The Lincolnshire Loop line runs into the city from the east and lies immediately to the south of the River Witham. Reproduced from 1930, 6 in. Ordnance Survey map revised 1938

An aerial view of Brayford Pool, Lincoln, taken in the early 1950s. In the foreground leading from Brayford pool are the mills, maltings and warehouses served by the working barges lining the navigation and the Brayford. At the centre foreground is the Great Northern Railway goods shed of 1876 with beyond it the locomotive shed and Lincoln Central station. To the right of the shed is the Great Central Railway's warehouse, built in 1907, with its sidings. To the right again is the Midland Railway goods shed, with St Marks station behind.

In September 1848, the MS&LR opened its line from Clarborough, near Retford to Saxilby Junction, near Lincoln. The GNR was granted running rights over the line in exchange for MS&LR running rights into Lincoln. This meant that trains could travel direct from Peterborough to Doncaster by way of Boston and Lincoln, joining the completed section of the GNR main line between Retford and Doncaster at Retford.

By an Act of 25th July, 1864, the GNR was, at last, able to complete the loop line by building its Gainsborough to Doncaster line. The Act also provided for the levelling of the old line between Sykes Junction and Gainsborough. This section, including the stations at Lea and Marton, was accordingly closed on 1st December, 1864, connection with Gainsborough being maintained via Retford. It was planned that the new line should cross the River Trent by a new bridge, but to save the considerable expense of such a structure, an agreement was made for the GNR to use the MS&LR bridge at Bole. This arrangement, and the necessary deviation, was sanctioned by an Act of 28th June, 1866.

The new line from Trent West Junction to Black Carr Junction, near Doncaster, as well as the rebuilt section from Sykes Junction to Trent East Junction, were opened to goods on 1st July, 1867, and to passengers two weeks later; the total distance amounted to 26 miles 36 chains. There were seven overbridges, nine underbridges and eleven viaducts, the most important being for the Trent floodwaters, which had 18½ spans of 30 ft.

Unusually heavy earthworks were required to keep the line level. Despite this there remained a long bank of 1 in 200 between Lea and Marton. The track was laid with 82lb. rail, these also replacing 72lb. rails on the reconstructed section. Marton and Lea stations were reopened, and new ones built at Gainsborough, Beckingham, Walkeringham, Misterton, Haxey and Finningley.

BR class '03' diesel shunter No. 03 021 propels its train over the River Witham at Lincoln. Compare this view with the 1947 view on page vii.   *Rev. G.B. Wise*

Table 5.   PETERBOROUGH (NORTH), SPALDING, BOSTON AND LINCOLN (L.N.E.) (via BOSTON).

WEEKDAYS.

		a.m.	a.m.	a.m.	FO a.m.	WO a.m.	TO a.m.	a.m.	a.m.	p.m.	SO p.m.	p.m.	A B p.m.	A p.m.	A H p.m.
LONDON (King's Cross)	dep.	...	2 33	...	7 15	7 15	7 15	8 45	...	...	...	...	4 0	...	5 45 110
Peterborough (North)	arr.	3 106	4 42	...	9 30	9 30	9 30	1050	...	1 35	1133	...	5 38	...	7 9 310
PETERBOROUGH (North)	dep.	3 106	45	...	9 30	9 30	9 30	1050	...	...	2 10	3 22	...	...	7 18
Peakirk	...	...	56	...	...	...	9 45	...	...	...	2 21	3 33	...	...	7 29
St. James Dep for Mkt Drp.	...	...	7	...	9 42	...	9 45	...	...	...	2 25	3 37	...	...	7 33
Littleworth	...	...	...	...	...	...	9 57	...	...	...	2 33	3 45	...	...	7 41
Spalding	arr.	3 32	17	...	9 55	9 55	10 2	1122	...	...	2 42	3 54	...	...	7 50 332
	dep.	3 38	21	...	9 57	9 57	...	1132	...	...	2 54	4 10	6 0	6 33	7 54 338
Surfleet	...	...	28	...	10 4	10 4	...	1139	...	...	3 1	4 17	6 3	...	8 1
Algarkirk & Sutterton	...	...	35	...	10 11	10 11	...	1146	...	...	3 7	4 24	...	...	8 8
Kirton	...	...	41	...	10 17	10 17	...	1152	...	...	3 15	4 30	...	...	8 14
Boston	arr.	3 57	49	...	10 25	10 25	...	1212	...	...	3 30	4 38	6 22	...	8 22 357
Langrick	...	...	...	...	...	...	...	1221	...	...	3 39	...	...	...	...
Dogdyke	...	...	6	...	9 46	...	...	1231	...	...	3 49	...	...	...	...
Tattershall	...	...	14	...	9 56	...	...	1234	...	...	3 52	...	...	...	...
Woodhall Junction	arr.	...	24	...	9 59	...	...	1244	...	...	4 4	...	6 27	...	...
	dep.	...	27	...	10 8	...	...	1249	...	...	4 4	...	6 55	7 36	...
Stixwould	...	...	30	...	10 18	...	...	1254	...	...	4 9	...	7 37	...	...
Southrey	...	...	34	...	10 23	...	...	1259	...	...	4 13	...	...	...	...
Bardney	...	...	37	...	10 23	...	...	1125	...	...	4 18	5 16	7 47	...	...
Five Mile House	...	...	45	...	10 25	...	1038	1126	...	...	4 24	5 20	6 31	7 48	...
Washingborough	...	...	51	...	10 33	...	1048	...	...	...	4 30	...	...	...	...
LINCOLN (L.N.E.)	arr.	9 1	59	...	1044	...	1057	1141	...	...	4 43	5 35	6 67	8 3	...

A   Restaurant Car King's Cross to Peterborough (North).
B   Through Train King's Cross to Grimsby Town, and Through Carriage King's Cross to Horncastle.

FO   Fridays only.
H   Sunday mornings excepted.
SO   Saturdays only.
SX   Saturdays excepted.

TO Tuesdays only.
WO Wednesdays only.

SUNDAYS.

		n.n 12.0	p.m.
LONDON (King's Cross) dep.		...	1 35
Peterborough (North) arr.		...	1 36
PETERBOROUGH (North) dep.		2 15	...
Peakirk		2 26	...
St. James Dep for Mkt Drp.		2 30	...
Littleworth		2 38	...
Spalding arr.		2 47	...
dep.		2 51	...
Surfleet		2 58	...
Algarkirk & Sutterton		3 5	...
Kirton		3 11	...
Boston arr.		3 19	...
Langrick		3 26	...
Dogdyke		3 35	...
Tattershall		3 45	...
Woodhall Junction arr.		3 48	...
dep.		3 55	...
Stixwould		3 56	...
Southrey		4 5	...
Bardney		4 10	...
Five Mile House		4 11	...
Washingborough		4 19	...
LINCOLN (L.N.E.) arr.		4 24	...
		4 32	...

WEEKDAYS.

		B a.m.	a.m.	a.m.	FO a.m.	a.m.	a.m.	C a.m.	a.m.	a.m.	p.m.	p.m.	p.m.	TO p.m.	WO p.m.	FO p.m.	p.m.	p.m.
LINCOLN (L.N.E.)	dep.	7 37	8 18	...	9 15	...	1120	1038	1240	1 5	...	3 19	3 5	1 45	...	...	3 47	...
Washingborough	...	7 45	...	...	...	...	1126	1044	...	1 16	...	3 21	...	1 53	...	...	...	...
Five Mile House	...	7 51	...	8 16	9 29	...	1136	1057	1254	1 24	...	3 31	...	...	2 28	...	...	...
Bardney	...	7 58	8 19	8 33	9 30	...	...	1110	1255	...	...	3 37	...	...	2 36	...	...	...
Southrey	...	...	...	...	...	...	...	1115	...	...	...	3 41	...	...	...	...	...	...
Stixwould	...	...	...	...	9 39	...	1146	1125	1 4	...	...	3 45	...	2 7	2 56	...	...	...
Woodhall Junction	arr.	...	8 25	...	9 41	...	1147	1128	1 6	...	...	3 48	...	2 11	2 59	...	...	...
	dep.	...	8 30	...	...	...	...	1125	...	...	...	3 16	...	...	3 12	...	...	...
Tattershall	...	...	8 35	...	...	...	...	1128	...	...	...	3 19	...	2 55	3 16	...	...	...
Dogdyke	...	...	8 42	...	9 54	...	...	1131	...	...	...	3 23	...	...	3 21	...	...	...
Langrick	...	...	8 45	...	10 14	...	...	1138	...	...	...	3 27	...	2 33	3 27	...	...	...
Boston	arr.	7 37	8 55	...	10 23	...	1147	1147	...	...	...	3 31	...	2 58	3 31	...	3 47	...
Kirton	...	7 45	9 4	...	...	1038	1157	...	...	...	...	3 34	...	...	...	...	3 50	...
Algarkirk & Sutterton	...	7 51	...	8 36	...	1044	...	12 5	...	...	...	3 39	...	...	...	...	5 10	...
Surfleet	...	7 58	9 0	8 39	...	1057	...	1218	...	...	...	3 46	...	...	...	...	...	...
Spalding	arr.	8 8	...	...	10 4	11 0	1218	1221	...	...	...	3 53	...	...	...	...	3 13	...
	dep.	8 18	9 0	...	10 4	11 0	1230	1230	...	...	...	6 6	...	2 55	...	...	...	...
Littleworth	...	8 26	...	...	10 4	...	...	1247	...	...	...	6 10	...	3 12	...	...	...	...
St. James Dep for Mkt Drp.	...	8 32	...	...	10 30	...	...	...	...	...	...	6 14	...	3 16	...	...	...	...
Peakirk	...	8 47	9 0	...	1030	...	1122	...	...	...	...	6 25	...	3 27	...	...	...	...
PETERBOROUGH (North)	arr.	9 12	9 12	...	1045	...	1138	1122	...	...	...	7 13	...	3 31	...	...	...	...
LONDON (King's Cross)	arr.	1040	1040	...	1230	...	1 53	1 53	...	...	...	...	...	4 30	...	5 10	...	...

A   Restaurant Car Peterborough (North) to King's Cross.
B   Mondays only.   Not after 27th October.
C   Through train from Grimsby Town and through carriage Horncastle to King's Cross.

E   Calls at Kirton Mondays to Fridays to set down only.   Calls on Saturdays at 9.45 p.m. to set down or take up passengers.
FO   Fridays only.
J   On Saturdays calls at Littleworth to set down passengers.

SUNDAYS.

		p.m.
LINCOLN (L.N.E.) dep.		5 43
Washingborough		5 49
Five Mile House		5 54
Bardney		6 4
Southrey		6 9
Stixwould		6 14
Woodhall Junction arr.		6 19
dep.		6 21
Tattershall		6 28
Dogdyke		6 31
Langrick		6 41
Boston arr.		6 50
dep.		7 0
Kirton		7 14
Algarkirk & Sutterton		7 21
Surfleet		7 28
Spalding arr.		7 31
dep.		7 40
Littleworth		7 48
St. James Dep for Mkt Drp.		7 53
Peakirk		8 5
PETERBOROUGH (North) arr.		8 35
LONDON (King's Cross) arr.		10.20

SO   Saturdays only.
TO   Tuesdays only.
WO   Wednesdays only.

Chapter Seven

Operation of the Line

The amount of traffic carried by the new railway during the first few months of its operation, exceeded all expectations. Five trains worked in each direction during the week with two on Sundays.

There were some operational problems during the early days. On the opening day of the line the last train from Lincoln to Boston ran through the crossing gates at London Road. The train, running over two hours late, was due at the crossing at 10.30 pm. At 11.00 pm the gatekeeper, having no orders to wait for a late train, left the gates across the line and went home. An hour and a half later the train crashed through the gates, fortunately with no injuries inflicted. The same gates were demolished on 3rd November, 1848, this time by a train running ahead of time.

Lack of information about the destination of trains created problems at Boston station; passengers for Hull found themselves in Lincoln with their luggage on its way to New Holland.

The Grand Sluice railway bridge was proving to be less than satisfactory. Up to 20 goods and passenger trains were using the single track bridge to gain access to the Loop line or the East Lincolnshire line. On a foggy morning in December 1849, the 11.15 am up train from Lincoln was approaching the bridge while a slow down luggage train was moving into a siding to allow it to pass. The up train hit the last four wagons of the luggage train, destroying them. Soon afterwards, in February 1850, new signals were installed at East Lincolnshire Junction, controlled from a cabin at Grand Sluice level crossing. In 1849 the GNR applied for permission from Parliament to make a deviation at the northern approach to the bridge, so as to eliminate the tight curve coming off the Loop. Tattershall Road was diverted to cross the ELR north of the junction, this being opened in April 1850. The new curve and the junction were inspected by Captain Laffau, on 2nd May, 1850, and brought into use on 12th.

Until the GNR main line opened from London, all GNR trains terminated at Peterborough. London connections were provided by services to Euston via the LNWR, or Shoreditch, over the Eastern Counties line.

On 5th August, 1850, a train carrying GNR Directors and their guests left the temporary station in London, situated just north of the site of Gasworks Tunnel, at Maiden Lane. The train left at 9.00 am bound for Peterborough. The formation was of 17 carriages worked by two engines. Stops were made at principal stations on the route and arrival at Peterborough was at 1.30 pm. On 7th August, the public opening took place, eight trains working in and out of London on weekdays, three on Sundays. On the 8th trains began to run to York. Although only a temporary terminus, Maiden Lane was already known as Kings Cross. John Carruthers was moved from Louth station to the job as station inspector at the terminus.

The GNR timetable dated 7th August, 1850, gives particulars of 10 up and 10 down trains on weekdays and four in each direction on Sundays. First, second

LOOP, LINCOLN TO BOSTON.

WEEK-DAYS.

			STATIONS.	1	2	3	4	5	6	7	8	9	10	11	12	13	14	15	16
Distance from Lincoln Station.	Distance Station to Station.			11.25 p.m. Coal Doncaster to Peterboro'.	Goods.	1.5 a.m. Coal Doncaster to New England.	Goods.	4.0 a.m. Coal Doncaster to New England.	Pass.	Goods to Horncastle.	Empty Coaches.	Pass. to Grantham.	Pass. to Skegness.	Pass. to Louth.	Pass. to Skegness.	9.10 a.m. Pass.	Horncastle.	6.40 a.m. Coal Doncaster to New England.	8.30 a.m. Exp. Pass. Sheffield to Skegness.	8.50 a.m. Pass. Doncaster to Peterboro'
M. C	M. C.		Class.	C	B	C	B	C		B							C			
					M	M	M		M			S								
			UP.	a.m. pass	a.m.	a.m. pass	a.m.	a.m. pass	a.m.	a.m.	a.m.	a.rn.	a.m.	a.m.	a.m.	a.m.	a.m. pass.	a.m.	a.m.
...	...		Lincoln Holmes Yd. ... dep.	1 13	2 30	2 46	5 15	3 51		6 45		...	...	...	...	...	8 45	...	...
...	0 44		,, Station ...... ,,	P'wype Jct.		P'wype Jct.	pass Jct.	P'wype Jct.	6 45			7 55		8 19	9 15		P'wype Jct. Via Avoid'n Line.	9 50	10 33
...			,, Pelham St.Jct. pass	1 23		2 56	5 30	6 1		6 57		8 1					9 31		10 40
...			Washingboro' Jct...... pass	...		...	...	...	6 51			8 1							10 46
2 43	2 43		Washingboro'............ dep.	...		...	...	...	6 57			8 6							10 50
5 18	2 55		Five Mile House .... ,,	1 W 53		3 W 26	6 ...	6 W 31	7 5	7 19		8 14		8 34	9 29		9 W 55	10 5	10 54
9 21	4 3		Bardney ....{ arr.	2 3		3 56	6 41			7 29		8 15		8 44	9 30		10 20	10 6	10 57
11 64	2 43		Southrey................... ,,				6 10					8 20							11 2
13 32	*1 48		Stixwould .... ,,				6 20					8 25							11 7
15 47	2 9		Woodhall Junction { arr.	2 27	3 23	4 20	6 28	6 50	7 55	9 35		8 30	8 40	9 39	9 27	pass	10 15	11 15
			{ dep.				6 50	7 5				8 35		9 41	9 45	10 44	10 17	11 15
Distance from Woodh'll			Coningsby Junction... pass				6 56					8 42		9 43	9 47		10 19	
June.			**DOWN.**															
4 28	2 70		Coningsby ....dep.				7 20					8 48		9 49				
6 69	2 41		Tumby Woodside ... ,,				7 43					8 53						
9 9	2 20		New Bolingbroke ... ,,				8 6					8 58		9 57				
11 28	2 19		Stickney .... ,,				8 35					9 4		10 3				
13 78	2 50		Midville .... ,,				9 16					9 10						
			Bellwater Junction pass				9 20					9 15		10 11				10 42
17 79	4 1		Little Steeping ...... dep.				9 28					9 18						pass
20 19	2 20		Firsby .... arr.									9 23		10 19				10 49
Distance from Lincoln			**UP.**															
19 10	3 49		Tattershall .... dep.									8 42		9 52				11 22
20 3	0 73		Dogdyke .... ,,									8 46		9 56				11 26
26 13	6 10		Langrick .... ,,									8 56		10 6				11 35
31 2	4 69		Boston Station .... arr.	3 17		5 10		7 15	9 5			10 16		11 45
31 40	0 38		,, Goods .... ,,		4 15			7 57				11 36		

STATIONS.	17	18	19	20	21	22	23	24	25	26	27	28	29	30	31	32	1	2
	Pass. to Grimsby.	Exp. Pass.	Pass. to Louth.	Goods.	Light Engine.	11.50 a.m. Goods Doncaster to New England.	Pass.	Workmen.	2.34 p.m. Pass. ex Doncaster.	Pass. to Skegness.	Goods.	Pass. to Skegness.	Pass.	Pass.	8.0 p.m. L.E. ex Horncastle.	9.30 p.m. Goods Doncaster Decoy to Peterboro'	Goods.	4.35 p.m. Pass. Doncaster to Peterboro'
Class.				D		B			A						A	B		
					S	FO	S							SO		SO		
UP.	a.m.	p.m.	p.m.	p.m.	p.m.	p.m.	p.m.	p.m.	p.m.	p.m.	p.m.	p.m.	p.m.	p.m.	p.m.	p.m. pass	a.m.	p.m.
Lincoln Holmes Yd. ... dep.	...	...	...	12 55	1 15		...	...	...						11 8		2 30	
,, Station ......,,	11 20	12 40	12 55	Via Avoid'ing Line		Via Avoiding Line.	3 5		4 2	4 15		6 10	6 30	10 25	6.33 p.m. working After	P'wype Jct.	2 35	5 58
,, Pelham St. Jct. pass	...	...	...	1 8		1 8		2 15								11 18		6 4
Washingboro' Jct. ...... pass	...	...	1 1	X					4 21		6 16		10 31				6 9
Washingboro'............. dep.	...	...	...	X		X			4 26		6 21		10 36				6 12
Five Mile House .... ,,	...	12 54	1 15	1 55			pass	3 20	4 17	4 34		6 29	6 44	10 44		11 W 48		6 17
Bardney ....{ arr.	...	12 55	1 25	3 28		2 38	3 22	4 19	4 38		6 30	6 47	10 45		12 5		6 19
,,e { dep.	...			3 45			3 27	4 24			6 35		10 50				6 24
Southrey .... ,,	...			4 5			3 32	4 29			6 38		10 55				6 29
Stixwould .... ,,	...			4 14	1 50		3 37	4 34	4 48		6 42	6 56	11 0				6 34
Woodhall Junction {arr.	11 43	1 4		5 20		2 59	3 40	4 39	4 51	5 15	6 43	6 59	8 25	12 29		3 23	6 36
{ dep.	11 45	1 5							4 53		6 45						
Coningsby Junction ... pass.	11 47																
DOWN.																	
Coningsby............... dep.	11 53							4 59		6 50						
Tumby Woodside ... ,,	11 58							5 4		6 55						
New Bolingbroke ... ,,	12 3							5 9		6 58						
Stickney .... ,,	12 9							5 15		7 5						
Midville............... ,,	12 15							5 21		7 12						
Bellwater Junction ... pass	12 20							5 26								
Little Steeping ...... dep.	12 23							5 29		7 23						
Firsby .... arr.	12 28							5 34								
UP.																
Tattershall .... dep.				6 20			3 48	4 46		5 45		7 6					6 43
Dogdyke .... ,,				6 25			3 52	4 50		5 55		7 16					6 47
Langrick .... ,,				7 35			4 2	5 0		6 25		7 18					6 57
Boston Station .... arr.			1 27				4 12	5 10				7 27		8 50	1 19		7 7
,, Goods .... ,,				7 58				4 54			6 41					4 15	

These pages are taken from the Working Time Table 11th July, 1927.

Distance from Boston Station. M. C.	Distance, Station to Station. M. C.	STATIONS.	1 12.0 mid. Empties, New England to Donc'st'r Mln. Yd. C M	2 Empty Coaches.	3 Empty Coaches, to Horncastle. S	4 Workmens.	5 Pass.	6 Pass. to Doncaster. HC	7 7.55 a.m. Pass. ex Skegness. FO	8 Pass.	9 9.50 a.m. Goods ex Louth.	10 6.30 a.m. Goods ex Peterboro'. B	11 Exp. Pass. HC	12 11.0 a.m. Pass. ex Grantham.	13 Goods. A	14 12.50 p.m. Pass. ex Skegness.
		DOWN.	a.m.	a.m.	a.m.	a.m.	a.m.	a.m.	a.m.	a.m.	a.m.	a.m.	a.m.	p.m.	p.m.	p.m.
...	0 38	Boston Goods .... dep.	1 12	...	...	...	...	...	...	7 52	...	9 40	...	9 45	...	...
4 69	4 69	,, Station ,,	...	...	6 25	7 0	...	...	...	8 1	...	9 49	...	10 50	12 12	...
10 79	6 10	Langrick ,,	...	...	...	...	...	...	...	8 11	...	9 59	...	...	12 21	...
11 72	0 73	Dogdyke ,,	...	...	...	...	...	...	...	8 15	...	10 3	...	10 30	12 31	...
Distance from Firsby		Tattershall ,,											11 8		12 35	
		UP.														
2 20	2 20	Firsby ,,	...	...	...	...	7 25	...	8 40	...	...	...	...	12 45	1 25
3 63	1 43	Little Steeping ,,	...	...	...	...	7 30	...	8 45	...	...	...	...	12 56	1 31
6 21	2 38	Bellwater Junction ... pass	...	...	...	...	7 33	...	8 48	...	...	...	...	1 32	1 36
8 71	2 50	Midville ... dep.	...	...	...	...	7 38	...	8 53	...	...	...	...	2 0	1 42
11 10	2 19	New Bolingbroke ,,	...	...	...	...	7 44	...	8 59	...	...	...	...	2 40	1 47
13 30	2 20	Tumby Woodside ,,	...	...	...	...	7 49	...	9 4	...	...	...	...	3 2	...
15 71	2 41	Coningsby ,,	...	...	...	...	7 55	...	9 10	...	...	...	...	3 25	1 55
18 61	2 70	Coningsby Junction ... pass	...	...	...	...	8 1	...	9 16	...	...	...	...	3 32	2 0
Distance from Boston								8 6		9 21						
		DOWN.														
15 41	3 49	Woodhall Junction { arr. { dep.	...	1 50	6 55 7 10	...	8 8	8 22 8 25	9 23 9 30	10 10 10 12	...	10 45 11 20	11 14 11 16	12 42 12 45	3 40 4 15	2 2 2 3
17 50	2 9	Stixwould ,,	...	...	...	...	...	8 30	...	10 17	...	...	12 50	...	...
19 18	1 48	Southrey ,,	...	...	...	...	...	8 35	...	10 23	...	...	12 55	...	...
21 61	2 43	Bardney { arr. { dep.	2 16 2 16	... 7 15	...	...	...	8 40 8 43	9 41 9 43	10 28 10 30	10 40 10 43	11 40 11 27	11 26 1 1	1 0 1 1	4 34 4 44	2 12 2 12
25 64	4 3	Five Mile House ,,	...	...	...	...	...	8 51	...	10 38	...	A	1 9	...	...
28 39	2 55	Washingboro' ,,	...	...	...	...	...	8 57	9 53	...	10 53	A	1 15	...	2 22
...	...	Washingboro' Junc. ... pass	...	...	...	...	...	...	...	...	...	12 5	...	5 6	...
...	...	Lincoln Pelham St. Jct. ... pass	2 44	...	...	...	...	...	...	...	...	...	...	...	...
31 2	2 43	,, Station .... arr.	...	7 35	...	...	...	9 8	10 3	10 50	11 2	11 45	1 25	...	2 32
31 46	0 44	Holmes Yard ,,	...	...	...	...	...	...	...	...	12 17	...	...	5 24	...
		Pyewipe Jct. and Yard ,,	3 0	...	...	...	...	...	...	...	...	...	...	...	...

Notes in columns: 6 HC; 10 B (Not to convey from Boston traffic for Doncaster and beyond); 8 Hall Hills arr. 7.6 a.m.; 5 E.T. leaves Engineers Yard 6.45 a.m.; 11 Via Greetwell; 14 Via Avoidg. Line.

STATIONS.	15 1.55 p.m. Exp. Pass. Skegness to Sheffield.	16 Goods. D	17 Pass.	18 2.30 p.m. Pass. ex Grimsby.	19 Empty Coaches.	20 5.33 p.m. Pass. ex Louth.	21 4.40 p.m. Pass. Peterboro' to Doncaster via Loop. HC	22 Pass. to Horncastle.	23 6.30 p.m. Pass. ex Skegness.	24 7.40 p.m. Goods ex Horncastle. A	25 Goods to Doncaster. A	26 9.45 p.m. Goods to Doncaster Decoy. A	27 Empty Coaches.	28 7.40 p.m. Goods New England to Doncaster Decoy. SO	29 8.55 p.m. Goods New England to Doncaster Decoy. 80	1 2.15 p.m. Pass. Peterboro' to Doncaster. S
DOWN.	p.m.	p.m.	p.m.	p.m.	p.m.	p.m.	p.m.	p.m.	p.m.	p.m.	p.m.	p.m.	p.m.	p.m.	p.m.
Boston Goods .... dep.	...	1 E20	...	...	4 30	...	...	...	...	...	8 15	9 45	...	10 24	10 38	3 21
,, Station ,,	...	...	3 34	...	Loco.	...	5 58	6 33	...				...			3 21
Langrick ,,	...	2 15	3 43	...	...	...	6 7	...	...		Bank to:		...			3 30
Dogdyke ,,	...	3 5	3 53	...	...	...	6 17	...	...				...			3 40
Tattershall ,,	...	4 35	3 57	...	...	...	6 21	...	...				...			3 44
UP.																
Firsby ,,	pass 2 10	...	...	4 23	...	...	...	6 55	...				...			
Little Steeping ,,	...	...	...	4 28	...	...	...	...	...				...			
Bellwater Junction ... pass	2 17	...	...	4 31	...	...	...	7 1	...		Via Greetwell Jct. or Sincil obtain best working.		...			
Midville ... dep.	...	...	...	4 36	...	...	...	7 7	...				...			
Stickney ,,	...	...	...	4 42	...	...	...	7 13	...				...			
New Bolingbroke ,,	...	...	...	4 47	...	...	...	7 19	...				...			
Tumby Woodside ,,	...	...	...	4 53	...	...	...	7 27	...				...			
Coningsby ,,	...	...	...	4 59	...	...	...	7 32	...				...			
Coningsby Junction ... pass	2 30	...	...	5 4	...	...	...	7 37	...				...			
DOWN.																
Woodhall Junction { arr. { dep.	2 38 2 40	4 50 5 40	4 5 4 8	5 6 5 8	...	...	6 28 6 32	6 55 7 3	7 39 7 40	8 1 8 21	pass 8 53	pass 10 23	11 5	pass 11 30	pass 11 16	3 52 3 55
Stixwould ,,	...	5 55	4 13	...	...	...	6 37	...	...				...			3 58
Southrey ,,	...	6 10	4 18	...	...	...	6 42	...	...				...			4 3
Bardney { arr. { dep.	2 48 2 49	6 19 6 45	4 23 4 27	5 18 5 20	...	6 23 6 28	6 47 6 48	7 50 7 51	...		W		11 45 11 58	11 W30 11 40	4 8 4 9
Five Mile House ,,	...	X	4 35	...	...	6 35	6 56	...	...				...			4 17
Washingboro' ,,	...	X	4 41	...	...	6 41	7 2	...	...				...			4 23
Washingboro' Junc. ... pass	...	...	...	...	...	...	...	...	8 55				12 20			
Lincoln Pelham St. Jct. ... pass	...	...	...	...	...	...	...	...	...		pass 9 48	pass 10 57			12 3	
,, Station .... arr.	3 5	...	4 50	5 34	...	6 51	7 13	...	8 12				11 35			4 31
Holmes Yard ,,	...	7 30	...	...	...	...	...	...	9 0		pass 9 53	11 0		pass 12 28	12 11	
Pyewipe Jct. and Yard ,,	...	...	...	...	...	...	...	...	...				...			

Notes: 16 Via Greetwell Jct. & Avoiding Line; 18 Hall Hills arr. 4.35 p.m.; 28/29 Via Avoidg. Line.

Column: **Sundays.**

E May be detained on Wednesdays until 2.0 p.m. for cattle traffic from Boston Market.
F Stops when necessary to detach wagons Important Goods for Branch Stations.

and third class fares were available. The quickest journey, starting from London at 6.00 pm arrived in York at 12.45 am, a time of 6 hours 45 minutes at an average speed just in excess of 15½ mph.

A passenger could leave Maiden Lane at 7.40 am and arrive in Edinburgh at 9.10 pm, a journey lasting 13½ hours. The train would have called at Hatfield, Hitchin, Biggleswade, Huntingdon and Peterborough (for 10 minutes at each station), Spalding, Boston, Kirkstead, Lincoln and Retford (for three minutes), Doncaster and Knottingley (for two minutes), Milford, the junction for Hull and Church Fenton, the junction for Harrogate, before arriving at York where it stayed for 13 minutes. Continuing northwards, calls were made at Darlington, Durham, Newcastle and Berwick before eventual arrival in Edinburgh, this journey achieved an average speed of 31 mph, including stops, and was a remarkable performance for the period. Alternatively the traveller might start his journey at either 6 am or 10.30 am and arrive at 4.55 am the following morning. On Sundays the one through train of the day started from London at 7 am and arrived in Edinburgh at 4.55 am the next day! The return journey from Edinburgh saw a weekday train leaving at 11.00 pm and arriving at Maiden Lane at 7.30 pm the next evening. Journeying by this train however, involved a four hour wait in York. There were no through connections from stations north of York on Sundays.

A passenger could not book straight through for places north of York but had to re-book on arrival at that place. No matter at what time an unfortunate third class ticket holder arrived at York from the North, he could only leave that place going south by the 9.45 am train.

A point of interest concerns many regulations which became standard practice and which were already established by 1850. Children under three years travelled free, those between three and twelve years for half fare. Day tickets costing one fare and a half for a double journey were issued at any stations on the line to first and second class passengers. Day tickets issued on a Saturday were available either on that day or on the following Sunday or Monday. Horses and carriages were conveyed to and from all first class stations, and 'passengers riding in their own carriages' had to pay the first class fare. Each first and second class traveller was allowed 100 lb. of luggage free, and each third class passenger 56 lb. Smoking was strictly prohibited at stations or in the carriages under a penalty of 40 shillings. No gratuity was permitted to be taken by anyone working on the railway company, 'under any circumstances'.

The first epoch of the GNR's north-south activity was concluded with the opening of the 'Towns' line, on 14th October, 1852. After this time the Loop line became much more localised in its activities.

When the Gainsborough extension opened in 1849, the passenger train service was four trains each way on weekdays and two trains each way on Sundays. The Sunday trains were discontinued in July 1863, because of low receipts. Towards the end of 1858 the Engineer suggested singling the line between Sykes Junction and Gainsborough because of disappointing traffic figures. Although the GNR Directors were in favour, their solicitors doubted the legality of such action.

Class 'J6' 0-6-0 No. 64181 enters Spalding with a freight from Peterborough in June 1956. The line in the foreground formed the branch to Bourne and those to the left to March. No. 64181 was fitted with a tablet catcher for working over the single line sections of the M&GN.

Peter Batty

Class 'V2' 2-6-2 No. 60872 *Kings Own Yorkshire Light Infantry*, on an up goods at Spalding on 23rd June, 1954.

Horace Gamble

Rebuilt GNR 2-2-2 No. 232 at East Lincoln Junction, Boston on 13th August, 1907.

Pilcher Collection, NRM

Large boilered 'Atlantic' 4-4-2 No. 251 with an experimental chimney designed by Bulleid, at Boston on 8th August, 1907. No. 251 is preserved as part of the National Collection.

Pilcher Collection, NRM

The MS&LR began to complain about the unpunctuality of GNR trains arriving at Gainsborough. Edward Bury was called upon to sort out the problem. He reported that engine No. 23 had leaky tubes and that No. 54's problems stemmed from bad water at Gainsborough. This water was not being used by MS&LR engines and the GNR soon found alternative supplies.

In May 1849 it was stipulated that GNR express trains should operate at a speed of 36 mph and ordinary trains at 30 mph, with 2½ minute stops. In order to standardise train timings, a master clock was provided at Boston, in July. Guards were to set their watches to railway time when working the first train of the day. They were responsible for communicating the information to all stations.

The following May, the GNR Directors' attention was called to a drop in passenger takings over the Loop as well as damage caused to banks of the River Witham by the river steamers. The new locomotive engineer, Archibald Sturrock, who had succeeded Bury, was instructed to convert six cattle wagons into passenger vehicles without seats. This was done at a cost of £7 10s. per wagon. One or more of these new vehicles were attached to slower trains working between Boston and Lincoln, the fare, described as 'fourth class', was charged at ½d. per mile. It was hoped that this would put paid to the river steamers, however it was a further 11 years before that happened; indeed, many passengers, having experienced 4th class travel, returned to the river steamers!

Problems arose concerning the siting of Lincoln station yard between two level crossings, only 430 yds apart. Pelham Street crossing was traversed by five tracks and High Street by two. Frequent, and often long, delays to the city's traffic, due to the gates being closed, brought a steady stream of complaints from the city authorities. The GNR was not at all responsive to the pleas from the City Council and in 1868 the matter was referred to the Board of Trade. Colonel Yolland investigated and discovered that the majority of hold ups at the crossings were caused by shunting movements. The GNR was informed that no shunting would be allowed over the crossings, after 1st January, 1870.

Problems at High Street crossing began almost as soon as the Loop opened. The *Lincolnshire Chronicle* reported, on 9th November, 1849:

On Friday morning last one of the gates at the High Street crossing of the GNR, was broken by the engine of a luggage train. It appeared that the train arrived in Lincoln before its time, the whistle was sounded as usual but because of fog the engine driver could not see whether the gates were open or not until within twenty yards of them, when he found it was too late to pull up, although every endevour was made to do so by use of the brakes. The gatekeeper, who is a very active man, got one of the gates open in time, and in endeavouring to open the one which was broken, very narrowly escaped being run over by the engine.

On 27th April, 1860, the newspaper reported:

A most fearful accident was, by the merest chance avoided at the High Street crossing of the GNR at about a quarter past four on Wednesday morning. A long train of horse boxes, having being brought into the station, were being shunted back, when, from some oversight on the part of the engine driver, who never operated the whistle, the

The 9.07 am Doncaster to Peterborough train, via Lincoln and Boston, at Boston in 1956. This train called at all stations. Class 'B17' 4-6-0 No. 61626 *Brancepeth Castle* is in charge. *Les Perrin*

Ivatt 'Mogul' No. 43060 arrives at Sleaford Junction, Boston with a freight train on 23rd June 1958. Notice the recess for the tablet catcher on the tender. *R.C. Riley*

wagons were upon the gates before Chambers, the gatekeeper was aware of their proximity. Cries were raised and Chambers ran to the gates, evidently with the intention of opening them, he was knocked down, his legs being under the gate and across the line, scarcely two feet from the front wheel of a wagon, however, his colleague, with admirable presence of mind turned him round as he lay and so further injury was averted.

The following year on 4th January, a further catastrophe was reported:

It appears that the down goods train arrived about half past ten o'clock in the station yard, but owing to the fact that the wagons were heavily laden, combined with the slippery state of the rails, the driver was unable to bring the train to a standstill in time and the engine ran through the massive protection gates at High Street crossing, smashing three of them to pieces and forcing the fourth back so that it was rendered useless. The force of the concussion may be imagined when we state that large pieces of the gate were hauled forward nearly as far as the Holmes bridge and nearly the whole of the ornamental vases on the terrace of the GNR Hotel were demolished by the splinters and broken bars of the gates.

Two reports in the *Lincolnshire Chronicle* in 1849 demonstrate that the GNR's baptism in Lincoln had its human as well as operational problems.

Great complaints are made in Lincoln of the want of courtesy and servility on the part of clerks and officials connected with the offices of the Great Northern Railway Company. Both in the parcels office and the passenger office great inservility and rudeness have been experienced by some of the most respected citizens.

And,

This unfortunate company seems doomed to be victimised. On Saturday night last, Mr Grimshaw, the Lincoln Superintendent of Porters, at Lincoln Station, decamped, carrying with him between £100 and £200 of the company's monies. It appears he has for some time had the management of the goods department, so far as relates to receiving monies for carriage and that his accounts were in arrears; instead of remaining to clear up any deficiencies, he has 'absquatulated', his wife and four children followed him on Monday night last.

It was decided to change the site of the turntable and extend the sidings on the Holmes to accommodate coal deliveries. The sidings were laid in 1868 and extended in 1870. Additional lines between Lincoln North and Brayford Mere were brought into use in May 1873. Initially the GNR Directors had refused to install watering facilities for goods and coal trains on the Holmes, but by 1874 these facilities were available.

By 1899 passenger trains over the Loop comprised two trains, working all stations between Peterborough and Doncaster, the 7.00 am from Peterborough, arriving at Doncaster at 11.02 am. This train called at Boston, at 8.04 am, where it collected mail bags for Langrick, it was also authorised to collect cattle from the Louth-Bardney branch at Bardney, provided the wagons were fitted with brake pipes. In fact most trains working over the Loop were allowed to collect

GNR '1031' series 0-6-0 No. 4033 departs Boston with a Peterborough-Lincoln goods on 29th September, 1926. Many of these engines were responsible for traffic between the West Riding, Doncaster and Peterborough via the Loop as well as local passenger trains.

LCGB/Ken Nunn Collection

Twin Composite Brake unit Nos. 44162/1 lettered 'Horncastle Branch' and seen here at Woodhall Junction in May 1954. The set was made up of the coach bodies of railmotors Nos. 5 and 6.

Author's Collection

cattle from specific stations, either daily, or at certain times of the week, usually coinciding with a market day at one of the major towns along the line.

Six wheel-coupled tender engines could haul up to 35 wagons of cattle, meat and goods over the Loop. For a general pick-up goods the limit was 45 wagons, and had to be accompanied by two guard's vans, unless otherwise arranged. Mineral trains and heavy goods trains were allowed either 39 or 49 wagons between April and October, and 35 and 45 during the period November to March, the amount of the load depending upon the size of the engine's cylinders. The limit for ironstone trains was 24 loaded and 55 empty.

The GNR management was always keen to promote new passenger traffic, one aspect of this being special trains. Certainly Lincolnshire, because of its seaside location, saw a lot of this kind of traffic during the summer months. Another important event for the GNR was the Doncaster St Leger race meeting; until the 'Towns' line was completed traffic from London for this event would travel over the Loop line. On 16th September, 1850 incompetence, bordering on the farcical, conspired to make the 10.45 am special from London 2½ hours late at Doncaster. The train engine a 'small Hawthorn' had a pilot attached at Peterborough which had a 'green fire', and as a result caused some delays. At Boston time was lost because of lack of steam. The replacement engines provided at Boston were not suitable for the job. 'Small Hawthorn' No. 57 had been filled with 'bad water' and primed so much that it could not work effectively; Sharp 'Single' No. 15, which had just been outshopped, could not work at high speed due to overheating. The Lincoln Pilot engine due to replace No. 15, had been sent away to shunt by the Lincoln station master and so was not available. After the debacle the GNR decided that five hours was not enough time for such a heavy train.

The *Lincolnshire Chronicle* carried a report about a special train on 29th January, 1858,

> Last Saturday the GNR started a cheap trip from Lincoln and all the important towns on the Lincolnshire Loop Line for London, on the occasion of the marriage of the Princess Royal of England. The passengers booked at Lincoln amounted to only 70 although the return fare was, first class 10s., covered carriage 6s. This affords ample proof of the scarcity of money and the depression of trade at this particular time of the year.

In July 1900 the GNR were offering 1, 2, 3, 4, 5 and 6 day trips to Blackpool, and back, from Hubberts Bridge, Boston, Horncastle, Louth, Lincoln and Gainsborough. The train left Hubberts Bridge at 5.00 am, on 23rd July, and arrived at Blackpool Central at 10.40 am. Connections were made with the Horncastle train at Kirkstead at 5.40 am, and with the Louth train at Bardney at 5.52 am. The train was made up of 12 vehicles, including carriage brakes and two saloons. One saloon was reserved for Hensman's party, and one for the Revd Clarke's party joining at Kirkstead. Mr Halliday, at Boston, provided the guards.

The GNR worked the trains between Boston and Kirkgate and the Lancashire and Yorkshire Railway between Kirkgate and Blackpool. Passenger holding 2, 3, 4, 5 or 6 day tickets could return from Blackpool by any ordinary train having

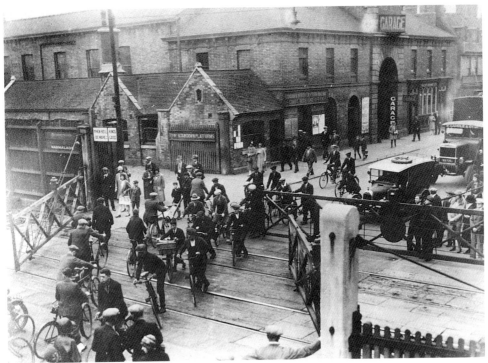

High Street crossing in Lincoln, in about 1932, showing the old GNR stable building which stood opposite the Great Northern Hotel. *D.N. Robinson Collection*

The elegant frontage of Lincoln Central station in 1950. *Author's Collection*

a through connection via Wakefield and Haxey.

On Wednesday, 25th July, a half-day trip from Lincoln, Bardney, Kirkstead to Boston and Skegness was advertised. The train left Lincoln at 2.00 pm, arriving at Boston at 2.51 pm, and Skegness at 3.36 pm. The return journey left Skegness at 8.10 pm, arriving back at Lincoln at 9.59 pm. Mr Reading, at Lincoln, was responsible for assessing the strength of the train and providing a guard. The outward special was worked from Boston to Skegness by the engine booked for the 3.38 pm ordinary timetable service, its train being taken forward by the engine off the special.

Also advertised was a half day trip from Lincoln to Woodhall Spa and Horncastle. Leaving Lincoln on the 2.00 pm special from Boston and Skegness, passengers arrived at Kirkstead at 2.27 pm, Woodhall Spa at 2.35 pm and Horncastle at 2.46 pm. The return trip left Horncastle at 6.09 pm arriving at Lincoln at 7.11 pm. Alternatively passengers could remain at Woodhall Spa and catch the returning Boston-Lincoln special at Kirkstead at 9.20 pm.

A bad accident occurred at Boston in October 1923, when the 4.40 pm down passenger train from Kings Cross was in collision with the station pilot. The situation was that in the up platform stood the 6.08 pm to Grantham. On the up main line a goods train was approaching. The pilot, a class 'D1' 4-4-0 No. 1384, was coming along the down main line in the up direction to pull off a wagon and the two London coaches. The driver of No. 1384 must have thought he was on the up main line rather than the down. The signals were on a gantry, with upper ones showing above the level of the bridge behind and lower (repeater) ones below, for better visibility. West Street signal box pulled off the up main signal and the pilot went forward and crashed head on with the class 'C1' 4-4-2, possibly No. 897.

During the General Strike of 1926, a fish train worked by an Atlantic type locomotive, was brought into Boston from Grimsby docks, crewed by a clergyman and two London University undergraduates. They had left the docks at 12.00 and arrived in Boston at 7.00 pm, having run through several sets of gates without opening them!

During the life of the Loop, train times, particularly in the 20th century, varied very little.

In the early 1920s a passenger train locomotive duty to Boston left Peterborough at 7.40 am, arriving in Boston at 8.43 am and departing for the return trip at 9.50 am. The train arrived at Peterborough at 10.58 am and a second crew took over, taking the 2.10 pm back to Boston where it arrived at 3.17 pm. The return working was the 6.55 pm to Peterborough, this connected with the 4.40 pm stopping train from Grimsby, which arrived at Boston at 6.48 pm. The Louth engine was taken off and the Peterborough Atlantic or 4-4-0 put on the train.

The 10.50 am express working from Boston to Lincoln ran daily, calling at Woodhall Junction and Bardney, returning at 1.27 pm. This train was worked by an Ivatt 0-6-0 which brought the 6.30 am goods to Boston from Peterborough arriving at Boston at 9.30 am, on its return from Lincoln the engine finally left Boston with the 4.00 pm goods to New England where it arrived at 8.47 pm (8.02 pm on Saturdays). The exception was on Wednesdays when a Boston

The notorious High Street crossing in Lincoln with an interesting collection of motive power in evidence, 14th October, 1952.   *Lincolnshire Echo*

Durham Ox crossing was arguably Lincoln's busiest crossing. Trains from the north, the east and south-east used it to gain access to Central and St Marks stations. In the 1950s work began on bridging the crossing. This photograph taken in April 1957 shows work progressing on Pelham Bridge.   *Lincolnshire Echo*

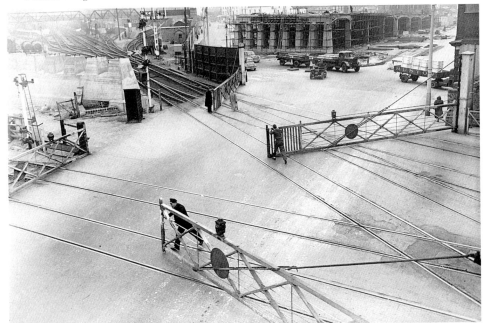

market train from Peterborough arrived in Boston at 10.25 am. The train engine then worked the return trip to Lincoln. On its return it worked the 2.28 pm to Peterborough.

On Tuesdays a market train for Spalding left Peterborough at 9.30 am, arriving at 10.30 am and returning at 2.35 pm.

A second 0-6-0 worked the 1.00 pm New England to Boston goods, arriving at 3.24 pm. The return working was at 5.15 pm, a stopping train to Peterborough arriving there at 6.20 pm. This engine returned to Boston, with a fresh crew, on the 7.18 pm passenger train. The engine would stand pilot and return to Peterborough on the midnight goods.

Boston Shed's most important duty was the 7.55 am stopping train to Doncaster via Lincoln, known as 'The Early Doncaster'. The return left Doncaster at 2.10 pm arriving at Boston at 5.07 pm. The train usually arrived in Boston behind the 3.00 pm from Grimsby, which arrived at 4.48 pm and departed after a refreshment stop at 5.12 pm. The Grimsby train pulled up to West Street crossing, allowing the Doncaster train to come in behind it.

There was a Doncaster turn which ran through to Peterborough via Lincoln and Boston, starting at 8.05 am and arriving in Peterborough at 1.00 pm. The crew then travelled home as passengers on a main line express. Another Doncaster crew, having travelled up as passengers to Peterborough, worked the engine home on the 4.40 pm reaching Doncaster at 8.39. Both trains called at all stations on the Loop.

The return Kings Cross to Doncaster working was an interesting one, the 4.40 pm from Kings Cross. This train was known as '261 Down Passenger'. '261' had one of the worst timekeeping records on the system. It was fine from Kings Cross as far as Peterborough at which point the two Boston coaches were backed on to the Doncaster train. After Peterborough the train would pick up fruit and flower traffic at Spalding, which often caused long delays during the season. The fruit was conveyed at the front of the train because of the necessity to detach the two through coaches from Kings Cross at the rear of the train, at Boston. Sometimes there would be a wagon or van on the rear, in which case the Boston pilot would come on to the rear of the train, take off the two coaches, place them on the down main line, and attach the wagon to the back of the train. The two coaches were moved into the bay until they left on the 6.55 pm for Grimsby, often with a Louth four car set. They would return to Boston the next day on the 12.40 pm from Grimsby.

With the exception of Saturdays, a 7.15 am passenger train ran to Peterborough, arriving at 8.23 am. The engine returned with a goods train at 12.50 pm. On Saturdays, the 9.37 pm mail was worked to Peterborough, where it arrived at 10.23 pm. The engine left at 2.30 am on Sunday morning with a goods train due in Boston at 5.00 am.

The first train from Lincoln was the 9.05 am worked by Lincoln men. The Lincoln engine, usually a class 'D1' 4-4-0 No. 1368, was taken off at Boston and stood station pilot, relieving an engine that had arrived from Bradford at 7.25 am; this latter engine took the Lincoln train on to Grantham. No. 1368 would await the arrival of a train from Grantham which arrived at 12.07 pm. Because a Peterborough to Grimsby train had arrived at 11.59 am and occupied the

Class 'J6' 0-6-0 No. 65016 leaves East Holmes Yard with a Lincoln-Boston goods in August 1950. No. 65016 was a Boston based engine. *Peter Batty*

Great Western Railway diesel railcar on trials between Lincoln and Boston on 9th October, 1952. The trials were to help ascertain the kind of diesel power required in Lincolnshire.
Lincolnshire Echo

down platform, the Grantham train ran straight through the station as far as the Sluice box and then came back into the bay. No. 1368 replaced the Grantham engine and took the train on to Lincoln at 12.12 pm, a quick changeover. The Grimsby train, worked by Louth men, departed at 12.15 pm.

The 3.30 pm Boston to Lincoln train connected with the 3.17 pm from Peterborough. The 3.30 was worked by Boston men, usually with a class 'D1' 4-4-0, usually Nos. 1356, 1358 or 1360. These three had retained small boilers and tall chimneys and were rebuilt to class 'D3' by the LNER in 1927/8. This train returned at 7.37 pm. It was usually held up at Boston by the Grimsby fish train, due around 7.36 pm. When the loading of fish trains was increased from 49 to 60 wagons the train would foul the Sluice crossing and the 7.37 had to come in behind it.

Boston was the depot for sacks which the GNR hired out to farmers for five shillings a week. The depot was on the end of the down platform. There were two sidings at the West Street end between the end of the down platform and West Street crossing, known as Sack Sidings.

The 6.45 pm to Horncastle first stood in Sack Sidings waiting until the down express had left, at which time it would come into the station before departing for Horncastle.

Sir Archibald Weigall lived in Woodhall Spa and was a friend of Queen Alexandra. The Queen and her daughter, Princess Helena Victoria, would often come and stay with the Weigalls. They travelled in a first class coach on the 4.00 pm from Kings Cross. The coach was stopped conveniently alongside the station master's office at Boston and the red carpet laid. The Queen and Princess would go into the station master's office, whilst the Horncastle train would come out of Sack Sidings and attach the first class coach, before taking it, and the Royal visitors, 'express' to Woodhall Junction and on to Woodhall Spa and Horncastle. Originally the engine returned light to Boston, working back to Horncastle with the 6.30 am parcels train the next morning. Later, however, it worked back into Boston on the 8.50 am from Horncastle.

Sir Archibald Weigall used his considerable influence with the GNR to get a through coach to Horncastle put on the 4.00 pm from Kings Cross, a most unusual arrangement. The Horncastle coach, along with the Grimsby and Cleethorpes coaches were detached at Peterborough. The coach was once again detached at Boston and taken to Horncastle by the 6.45 pm train.

In the summer of 1919 on Wednesdays and Fridays only, the 4.00 pm from Kings Cross would include a through coach for Woodhall Spa, 'only on request at Kings Cross by holders of tickets to Kirkstead (Woodhall Junction) or Woodhall Spa'.

After World War I Horncastle was served by a connection off the 3.00 pm Kings Cross to Cromer express. The coach was attached to the front of the train at Kings Cross. Upon arrival at Peterborough, the coach would be picked up by the 4.40 pm train which drew out of a bay platform and backed onto the Cromer train to attach the Horncastle coach and take it on to Boston, eventually arriving at Horncastle at 6.50 pm.

In June 1922 the GNR restored the daily Horncastle through coach on the 4.00 pm from Kings Cross, with a corresponding return service, which ran

Thompson class 'B1' 4-6-0 No. 61089 awaits a turn of duty outside Lincoln shed, Holmes Yard on 22nd October, 1962., two years before the shed closed.   *M. Whatmough*

Class 'K3' 2-6-0 No. 618654 seen here with a GNR tender at Lincoln in 1957, note the group of train spotters on the far platform. The 'K3' was a development of the Gresley GNR design introduced in 1924.   *Peter Washbourn*

throughout the year. The coach was worked with the Grimsby portion of the train. The through coach remained at Horncastle overnight. Next morning a parcels train left Boston at 6.25 am, the engine returning to Boston at 10.16 am, with the through coach, which was then attached to the up express. This service was advertised up until July 1931. After this time a connecting service between Horncastle and Boston operated. The through coach was reinstated on the 4.00 pm Fridays and Saturdays only in the summers of 1936 and 1937 with return through workings on Mondays and Saturdays. A separate 4.05 pm departure from Kings Cross for Cleethorpes and Skegness appeared from the summer of 1937, on Fridays and Saturdays, and included the Horncastle coach. The time for the total journey in 1939 was 3 hours 23 minutes compared with 3 hours 10 minutes in 1914.

In the 1930s there was an up goods train from Doncaster to New England which went through Boston, where it stopped for water. It was usually a long train often pulled by 'hospital engines' - engines which had just been overhauled or repaired and were running-in.

Some of the heavy trains leaving Boston for the North had to be banked up Sluice bank. In the 1920s the Ellerman Lines ran trains from Kings Cross to Immingham for cruises to the Midnight Sun. Two trains left Kings Cross; the first was a third class train which departed at 12.20 pm and the second a first class which left at 12.30 pm. On one particular occasion the leading train was unable to get started out of Boston station. West Street signal box thought he was leaving and let the first class train in behind. The driver of the first class gave two crows answered by his struggling colleague, whereupon the rear engine and train banked the third class train out of the station.

On Sundays, the return working of the 10.00 am Grimsby to Peterborough train left Peterborough at 2.15 pm, double-headed by a Peterborough engine as far as Boston. The Peterborough engine worked the 3.21 pm from Boston to Lincoln, arriving there at 4.31 pm. The engines return working was the 5.48 pm, reaching Peterborough at 8.15 pm.

The 2.15 pm from Peterborough had a Lincoln to Doncaster section worked by a Doncaster crew who had previously worked a GN-GE Joint express to Liverpool Street from Doncaster.

A Lincoln crew worked the 4.20 pm Doncaster to Lincoln arriving at 5.48 pm. This crew had worked down on a Liverpool Street to Doncaster express.

With the introduction of diesels railcars in 1959, the timetable showed seven up trains and five down, between Boston and Lincoln. The 10.27 am from Lincoln was, by this time, the only advertised steam-hauled train operating along the line during the week, although both the up and the down Sunday trains were steam-hauled. Special cheap day return tickets cost 7s. 5d. A three-monthly season ticket for journeys between Boston and Lincoln cost £14 4s. 3d.

A particular feature of the Loop line was the fishermen's specials, which ran for many years, bringing anglers from Yorkshire to fish in the River Witham at weekends. The trains ran from Wadsley Bridge and Sheffield Victoria, to Bardney, Southrey, Stixwould, Kirkstead, Tattershall, Dogdyke, Langrick and Boston, and back. At least once a season, a train of railwaymen from a Doncaster angling club visited the Witham, however, unlike the other trains,

Top: Class 'B16' 4-6-0 No. 61444 crosses High Street crossing and approaches Lincoln Central station on 2nd September, 1955.

R.M. Casserley

Centre: Pyewipe Junction and signal box, Lincoln on 15th March, 1947. *H.C. Casserley*

Right: Greetwell Junction signal box in 1983 which controlled the Washingborough spur off the GNR loop at its junction with the GN & GE Joint and also the point where the avoiding line left the lines running through the town area of Lincoln. *Peter Grey*

this one was authorised to set down between stations.

On 22nd July, 1900, the GNR ran what was described as a 1, 2, 3 day Fishermen's trip. The train travelled from Sheffield Victoria at 7.30 am, calling at Darnall, Woodhouse, Retford, Crow Park, Carlton and Lincoln, where the train arrived at 9.40 am. From here it ran through to Boston, stopping at stations along the way to drop off anglers.

The return journey set out from Boston at 4.07 pm, arriving back at Sheffield Victoria at 7.34 pm. The trains were formed of 10 third class coaches and two brakes. The engine, coaches and men remained at Sheffield during Sunday night to work the Monday special. Barkstone North and East and Honington signal boxes were required to be open for the passing of these trains. The popularity of angling amongst the workmen of Sheffield can be gauged when the membership of one single club, the Sheffield Amalgated Anglers Society, stood at 15,000 members. The *Picture Post* magazine described a day out on the Witham with a group of Sheffield fishermen.

Sheffield itself has one river and a canal. I doubt if it has any fish. But Sheffield can number its anglers in thousands, miners and steelmakers, silversmiths and forgemen, cutlers and grinders and greengrocers and butchers and clerks, in fact almost everybody who can persuade 't' auld lass' that her her husband is better out of the way than hanging round the house of a Sunday.

In 'pleasure fishing' you pick your own bit of water and move, if you think there's a better stretch down river. In 'match fishing' there's a draw for positions, and numbered pegs along the bank show each angler the water allotted to him. In a big match, with competitors lining the bank for half a mile or more, a maroon is sometimes used as a starting signal.

But fishing in a match starts long before the signal to begin fishing. It really starts as soon as a man has entered his name for it. From then on his spare time is devoted to the job. Home from the steelworks, where he handles tons of white hot metal at a time, a forgeman gets down to work of another kind, building a new float, perhaps, replacing a worn silk whipping on the slender top joint of a match rod, or overhauling his best line, made of nylon that it is not much thicker than a human hair. These men who earn there living heaving coal or melting steel, pride themselves at home on work so fine, that it would make the work of a skilled embroideress or a filigree jeweller look almost clumsy by comparison.

Perhaps that is one of the great attractions of preparations for angling, the contrast it offers to the normal heavy work of the day. And then when Sunday comes there's the quiet of it all, away by the riverside, with the roar and the heat and the smoke of the factory left behind. Angling here is more than a sport. It's a way to health, and in the past when factory conditions were worse than they are today it has helped many a Sheffield cutlery grinder to combat the effects of breathing dust, which at one time, was expected to put an end to his working life in his forties.

By 1965 two return trains ran on Saturdays and Sundays between Sheffield and Woodhall Junction, (Kirkstead). The fare was 15s. 6d. return. By this time fishermen were also travelling to the Witham by coach. During the 1950s a bridge, constructed from sleepers, crossed Billinghay Skirth at the point it emptied into the Witham, near Tattershall. During the week the bridge was patrolled by two railway policemen, whose job it was to enforce the axle loading restriction imposed upon vehicles using the bridge, mainly farm traffic.

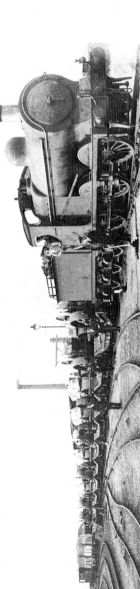

Above: Class 'J11' 0-6-0 No. 302 with its GCR number plates still in evidence a year after the grouping. The LNER renumbered the engine 5302 and it was one of 31 of its type rebuilt by Thompson in 1943 with piston valves and new cylinders. Seen here with a train load of tractors for Greece from Marshalls of Gainsborough.

Author's Collection

Right: The fisherman's specials went back a long way! The special detailed here ran on 22nd July, 1900.

Sheffield, &c., to Bardney, Southrey, Stixwould, Kirkstead, Tattershall, Dogdyke, Langrick, and Boston and back.

(Fisherman's 1, 2 or 3 days' trip.)

		3
		A.M.
Sheffield (Victoria)	dep.	b.7 30
Darnall	,,	7 37
Woodhouse	,,	7 43
Retford	arr.	8 13
Retford	dep.	8 18
Crow Park	,,	8 32
Carlton	,,	8 36
Newark		
Barkstone North Junction East	pass	8 47
Hougham Junction		9 7
Newark Junction		9 38
Lincoln	arr.	9 40
Lincoln	dep.	9 50
Bardney	,,	10 6
Southrey	,,	10 13
Stixwould	,,	10 19
Kirkstead	,,	10 25
Tattershall	,,	10 33
Dogdyke	,,	10 38
Langrick	,,	10 48
Boston	arr.	10 58

Empty train, engine to run tender first.

		4	3
		A.M.	P.M.
Boston	dep.		4 7
Langrick	,,		4 17
Dogdyke	,,		4 27
Tattershall	,,		4 31
Kirkstead	,,		4 39
Stixwould	,,		4 45
Southrey	,,		4 51
Bardney	,,		4 57
Lincoln	arr.		5 13
Lincoln	dep.		5 23
Navenby Junction			
Barkstone Road Junction	pass		
Newark North			
Carlton	dep.		6 24
Crow Park	,,		6 28
Retford	arr.		6 42
Retford	dep.		6 47
Woodhouse	,,	5 30	7 11
Darnall	arr. { Collect Sheffield tickets }		7 22
Darnall	dep.		7 57
Sheffield (Victoria)	arr.	6 10	7 34

To be 10 thirds and 2 carriage brakes, Mr. Wood, Retford, to provide guard. Mr. Wood, Retford, Reading, Lincoln and Shaw, and Halliday, Boston, how train is loaded.

A *return of tickets collected to be sent Superintendent of the line same day.*

Passengers booked Saturday also travel by return train.

Engine, coaches and men will remain at Sheffield during Sunday night to work Monday special.

Barkstone North and East and Honington signal boxes to be open for passing of these trains.

Tickets may be issued from Lincoln to Bardney by this train.

British Railways

ANGLERS' EXCURSIONS

SATURDAYS & SUNDAYS
20th JUNE to 6th SEPTEMBER 1964

GAINSBOROUGH SAXILBY LINCOLN BARDNEY
SOUTHREY STIXWOULD WOODHALL JUNCTION

Outward Journey

		Saturdays	Saturdays	Sundays	Sundays	Sundays
		a.m.	a.m.	a.m.	a.m.	a.m.
Wadsley Bridge	... ... dep.	—	6 30	•	6 2	—
Sheffield (Victoria)	... ... ,,	6 21	6 42	5 45	6 15	6 40
Darnall	... ... ,,	6 25	6 49	5 53	6 24	6 48
Woodhouse	... ... ,,	6 33	6 56	6 2	6 32	—
Kiveton Bridge	... ... ,,	6 42	—	—	6 42	—
Worksop	... ... ,,	6 57	—	—	—	—
Retford	... ... ,,	7 13	—	—	—	—
Gainsborough (Lea Road)	... ... ,,	7 27	—	—	—	—
Saxilby	... ... arr.	7 40	7 56	7 3	7 42	7 55
Lincoln (Central)	... ... ,,	7 53	—	—	7 59	8 12
Bardney	... ... ,,	—	8 29	7 42	8 26	8 39
Southrey	... ... ,,	—	8 37	7 50	8 34	8 47
Stixwould	... ... ,,	—	8 44	7 57	8 41	8 54
Woodhall Junction	... ... ,,	—	8 53	8 6	8 50	9 3

Return Journey

		Saturdays	Saturdays	Sundays	Sundays	Sundays
		p.m.	p.m.	p.m.	p.m.	p.m.
Woodhall Junction	... ... dep.	4 58	6 20	4 55	5 20	5 49
Stixwould	... ... ,,	5 3	6 29	5 4	5 29	5 58
Southrey	... ... ,,	5 7	6 37	5 12	5 37	6 6
Bardney	... ... ,,	5 13	6 48	5 22	5 47	6 16
Lincoln (Central)	... ... ,,	5 37	7 17	—	—	6 42
Saxilby	... ... ,,	5 46	7 27	5 57	6 22	6 55
Gainsborough (Lea Road)	... ... arr.	6 1	—	—	—	—
Retford	... ... ,,	6 20	—	—	—	—
Worksop	... ... ,,	6 33	—	—	7 6	—
Kiveton Bridge	... ... ,,	6 49	—	—	7 22	—
Woodhouse	... ... ,,	—	8 31	7 1	7 31	—
Darnall	... ... ,,	—	8 40	7 10	7 40	8 4
Sheffield (Victoria)	... ... ,,	—	8 48	7 17	7 47	8 11
Wadsley Bridge	... ... ,,	—	9 2	—	—	8 24

•—Will not run on Sunday 16th August

	Return fares second class						
	Gains-boro	Saxilby	Lincoln	Bardney	Southrey	Stixwould	Woodhall Junction
	s. d.	s. d.	s. d.	s. d.	s. d.	s. d.	s. d.
Wadsley Bridge	6/3	7/-	8/-	9/3	10/-	10/3	10/6
Sheffield	6/3	7/-	8/-	9/3	10/-	10/3	10/6
Darnall	6/3	7/-	8/-	9/3	10/-	10/3	10/6
Woodhouse	6/-	6/6	7/3	8/9	9/3	9/9	10/-
Kiveton Bridge	...	6/-	6/9	8/9	8/9	9/9	10/-
Worksop	...	5/6	6/3	8/3	9/-	9/-	9/6
Retford	...	4/6	5/3	7/6	8/3	8/6	8/9
Gainsborough	...	3/3	4/9	7/-	7/9	7/9	8/-

Services to Thorne, Crowne, Althorpe and Brigg overleaf

However at the weekends with no police on duty coaches loaded with fishermen and crates of beer crossed and recrossed the bridge with impunity.

Perhaps the most unusual train to visit the area was Barnum and Bailey's 'Greatest Show on Earth'. The world's largest circus spent two years touring Britain, travelling by train, covering 7,000 miles, and visiting 183 cities and towns. Lincoln was visited on 8th August, 1898, and Boston, Spalding and Gainsborough the following year.

The circus trains consisted of a total of 68 bright yellow carriages, each 54 ft in length, with red lettering proclaiming, 'Barnum and Bailey, Greatest Show on Earth'. The train also included box cars, each one capable of carrying 17 elephants or 25 horses. Daily transport costs alone during the tour amounted to £1,500 a day.

Four long trains arrived at the destination at hourly intervals throughout the night and early hours of the morning. Each section was shunted into specially cleared sidings, the operation overseen by the local district railway superintendent. The last train to arrive carried the huge canvases for the big top as well as 400 workmen, deck-polers, hook-teams and long-teams.

The performers arrived by a special train of sleeping cars, which also included the superb coach owned by James Bailey, the circus' owner; his partner Phineas T. Barnum, had died several years prior to the British tour.

The circus carried out two performances in each town. As the second performance was underway the tent riggers began striking the outer tents which included the restaurant tent, the stable tent, which accommodated 420 working and performing horses and the menagerie tent, which housed 100 animal cages, and moved them back to the railway sidings. By the time the performance ended all that remained was the Big Top itself.

Trains had been leaving at intervals during the final performance, on their way to the next venue. The circus agent paid off the railway workers for their part in a remarkable 24 hour operation.

A TRUTHFUL GROUND PLAN REPRESENTATION OF THE GREAT BARNUM AND BAILEY SHOW. AND VAST HIPPODROME TRACK 3 RINGS, 3 STAGES AND UPON WHICH IS PRESENTED ALL THE MODERN MODES OF LOCOMOTION WITH UP TO DATE COSTUMES, TYPICAL OF THE HORSELESS AGE.

Chapter Eight

Early Signalling

During the early days of the Loop, signals were operated by a lever attached to the signal post. It was not long, however, before the grouping of signal operating levers together in huts became common practice. Some of these structures were pretty primitive and little more than a roof. The term 'box' was being used by the end of the 1840s.

Early signalling provision at stations was soon found to be inadequate in dealing with the increasing volume of traffic. During the 1860s intermediate block posts began to appear.

A 'signal stage' at Spalding was described by the *Stamford Mercury*, on 4th May, 1866 as,

> .... principally of iron, consisting of a wooden stage 90 ft by 16 ft, supported by eight massive iron pillars 30 ft in height, put on 4½ cubic feet blocks of stone as bases. This stage is surrounded by a trellis work fencing of iron, 5 ft in height, which gives it a light and pleasing appearance. In the middle of the stage, immediately over the centre opening, is a handsome lookout, constructed of wood and glass with a leaden roof exhibiting great taste. Under the stage there are three 30 ft openings, a centre and two wings, through which the various trains pass. Midway between each couplet of pillars is a lofty iron patent signal by Stevens and Son. These signals graduate from 70 ft to 60 ft and have a light and pleasing aspect. The whole is very tastily constructed and reflects great credit on the contractors.

A new signal station was planned for Durham Ox Junction, (Pelham Street), in Lincoln in 1867, following a decision by the GNR to divert all mineral traffic through Lincoln from 1st March of that year. The decision was taken in the light of the imminent opening of the Honnington line and to relieve the main line. The scheme was completed by August and reported in the *Lincoln and Stamford Mercury*:

> The points and signals at Durham Ox crossing were finally inspected and approved by Captain Tyler on the 1st. The machinery is very elaborate and complete and embodies several new and ingenious ideas, the invention of Mr Brown, one of the Signal Inspectors of the GN line. One important improvement is that the points are worked before the signal is given and another that the working of one set of points simultaneously locks all the other points, so that a hostile train cannot approach. The machinery also works a small red disc, which rises out of a box at the foot of some signals, for the purpose of scotching an engine and it, like the points, is also worked before the signal is given. There is also a contrivance called a compensating lever by which the chains are either tightened or slackened in a moment, without leaving the signal house, according as the temperature renders it necessary and which ensures the perfect working of the signals. By this a chain can be let out or taken in two feet. There are 33 levers on the upper floor of the house and underneath is the machinery: these levers work 11 sets of points, 2 scotches and 24 signals, extending to a distance of 900 yards.

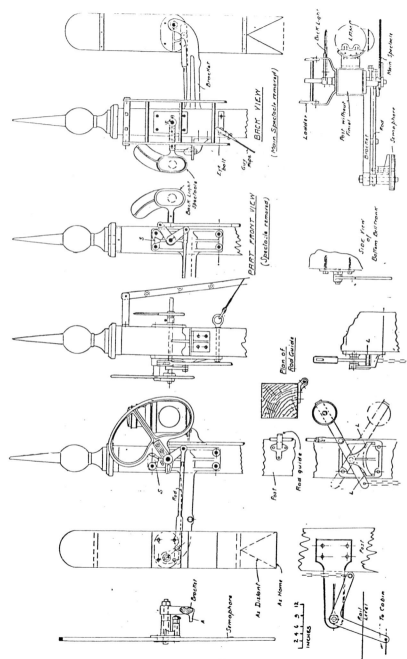

This drawing of a somersault signal was produced originally in Model Railways, August 1910.

11

Chapter Nine

Intermediate Stations

Without exception the intermediate stations along the Loop line served agricultural communities, surrounded by huge stretches of open countryside, the majority of which was flat fenland. The generally straight running between Peterborough and Boston, gave way to a series of abrupt curves as the line followed the course of the River Witham towards Lincoln.

With the opening of the Horncastle Railway in 1855 and the Louth and Lincoln in 1876, Kirkstead (later Woodhall) and Bardney became junction stations, each gaining an extra platform in the process.

Station buildings along the line were (and are) an example of early GNR architecture. Curious square three storey Italianate towers, with a pyramidal roof and round-headed windows were a feature at Peakirk, Spalding, Tattershall, Woodhall and Bardney. These were by no means uniform in style or construction. At Bardney and Woodhall Junction, huge ornate chimneys sat above the oddly chamfered roofs. Yellow bricks were used to build the Italianate buildings, with the exception of Woodhall Junction which was constructed of red bricks with yellow used a means of providing a decorative relief. The tower at Dogdyke was a less imposing version of the earlier ones. Red bricks were used to build the lesser stations, except at St James Deeping which was served by a half-timbered cottage. The contrast between the provision at this important place with that at the tiny village of Langrick is interesting. The building at Langrick was a solid structure with a strange little pantiled belfry.

Apart from Peterborough, Boston and Lincoln, the two most important stations along the line were at Spalding and Gainsborough.

Peakirk

Originally named 'Peakirk and Deeping', this was changed in 1851 to 'Peakirk for Crowland'. Peakirk was the first station beyond Peterborough and Werrington Junction on the Loop's northwards journey. The platforms here were staggered, with the station building and its Italianate three storey tower on the down side. A further section, away from the platform, had two storeys. The main siding ran round the back on the up side and the signal box was at the Peterborough end of the up platform. Jim Cuthbert a Peterborough top link driver recalled hundreds of tons of potatoes being sent to Scotland, 'where they were grown once and the seed sent back to England as the first scotch, the finest seed in the world'.

St James Deeping

Originally named 'Crowland and St James Deeping' this was changed to 'St James Deeping' in 1851. It remained so from that time on, apart from an entry

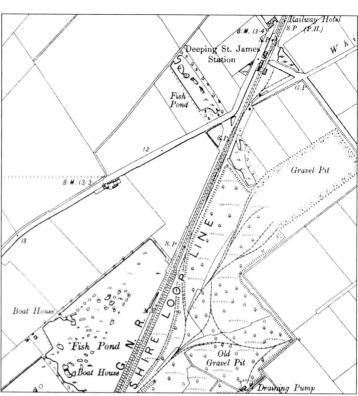

Right: Deeping St James station.
Reproduced from the 1901 6 in., Ordnance Survey map

Below Left: Peakirk station.
Reproduced from the 1899 6 in. Ordnance Survey map revised 1938

Below Right: Littleworth station.
Reproduced from the Provisional Edition 6 in., Ordnance Survey map

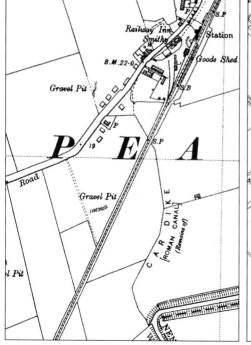

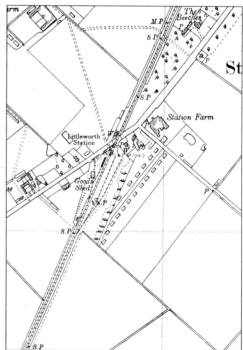

Peakirk station in 1952, note the staggered platforms.   *Author's Collection*

Littleworth signal box and crossing, looking towards Peterborough, 1981.   *N.D. Mundy*

The fireman of LNER class 'J3' 0-6-0 No. 4109 watches the driver of petrol tractor 'Billy' attend to his engine at the bottom of the ramp leading to the loading dock at Littleworth, 21st April, 1926.
Author's Collection

Spalding station showing the GNR lines and a good line-up of staff and station trolleys. An M&GN locomotive stands in the platform.
D.N. Robinson Collection

in *Bradshaw* for May 1923 when it appeared as 'Deeping St James'.
The layout here was similar to that at Peakirk, but without the staggered platforms. There were sidings on both sides of the line. One was provided for the use of ballast trains, around the back of the up platform. This was operated as follows: when a ballast train required to enter the siding the man in charge informed the signalman by one stroke of the gong in the signal box. The signalman would immediately unlock the points and sound the gong at the siding once. Once the train was clear of the main line, the gong in the box was sounded twice, informing the signalman that the line was clear. When the train required to regain the main line the signalman was informed by three strokes of the signal box gong. He replied with one stroke when all was ready for the train to leave the siding. Four strokes of the signal box gong informed the signalman that the ballast train was back on the main line. The gongs were used because of the distances between the shunter and signalman.

The main traffic here, as at Peakirk, was potatoes. The GNR at one time had a brickworks here.

Littleworth

One of the largest potato growers in the area, W. Dennis & Sons Ltd, had a private siding to the north of Littleworth station. This was the terminus of a 2 ft gauge railway which covered over 20 miles of Dennis' estate and was operated by a small petrol driven tractor called *Billy*. The railway enabled business on the estate to continue when the country roads in the area were waterlogged. Other farms in the area had their own railway systems, mainly worked by horses. Trucks pulled off the fields were unloaded into horse-drawn road wagons, by virtue of a specially constructed loading dock, built in the farm yard. From here the load would be taken to Littleworth station.

The potato traffic was seasonal, July and August being their busiest months. At the beginning of the season six or seven special trains a day would leave Littleworth loading dock, while the regular vegetable train, carrying potatoes for Peterborough and London, ran in six portions. At busy periods between 200 and 400 wagons of potatoes were despatched daily from Littleworth. Boston and Spalding were the principal despatch centres for potato traffic.

Hawthorn Bank signal box, between Littleworth and Spalding, was a block post. Jim Cuthbert remembered that when working nights, he often had to stop the train and walk to the box to wake up the signalman.

Spalding

In 1695 the merchants and traders of Spalding petitioned to have the town made a free port; the bid was unsuccessful and Spalding remained under the jurisdiction of the Port of Boston. After the first enclosure and drainage of the fens the River Welland was made navigable as far as Stamford, with the result that Spalding enjoyed an extensive trade in wool, coal and timber. Barges and sloops of about 50 to 60 tons came up to the centre of the town.

In 1824, two steam engines were erected to help improve the drainage of

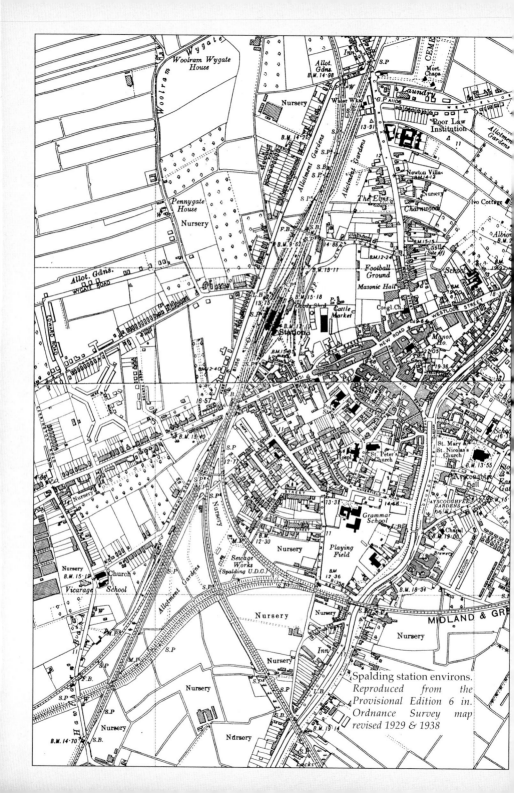

Spalding station environs.
Reproduced from the Provisional Edition 6 in. Ordnance Survey map revised 1929 & 1938

An M&GN class 'D' 0-6-0 takes water at Spalding station in about 1910. The extent of the station is well shown in this photograph with five trains in evidence. The original station buildings are on the right near the footbridge.   *D.N. Robinson Collection*

Spalding station looking towards Peterborough on 17th July, 1976.   *N.D. Mundy*

M&GN Johnson class 'C' 4-40 No. 48 stands in front of Spalding shed in May 1937. This is a good view of the shed's two through roads. *Author's Collection*

Another view of Spalding engine shed with LNER class 'J6' 0-6-0 No. 4217 standing alongside the ash pits in May 1948. *R.A.S.*

Class 'J20' No. 8288 on a goods train bound for March, at Spalding. Built by the GER in December 1922, No. 8288 was withdrawn in August 1960. The majority of these engines were allocated to Cambridge and March sheds, working heavy coal trains and very occasionally used on passenger work. *R.K. Blencowe Collection*

Ex-GCR class '04' 2-8-0 takes a goods train through Spalding station in 1929. *Author's Collection*

Ex-GCR class 'B5' 4-6-0 No. 5187 with the 11.32 am Doncaster-March train stands alongside ex-GNR class 'C1' 4-4-2 No. 4407 with the 12.40 pm Grimsby-Kings Cross service at Spalding station on 16th September, 1933. *H.C. Casserley*

M&GN class 'DA' 0-6-0 No. 86 runs a short train of cattle wagons through Spalding on 8th June, 1926. This is one of twelve Ivatt designed engines bought by the M&GN in 1900, No. 86 is seen here in original condition still with its smaller boiler. *H.C. Casserley*

Class 'J19' No. 8145 with a goods train bound for March, takes water at Spalding. Fitted with vacuum ejectors when constructed by the GER *c*. 1916, these engines were able to work fitted goods trains. Allocated to East Anglian sheds they were used on cross-country goods trains.

R.K. Blencowe Collection

Class 'B17/1' 4-6-0 No. 61626 *Brancepath Castle* with an express passenger train at Spalding on 4th March, 1950.

P.H. Wells

Deeping Fen, followed in 1830 and 1833 by a further two, to assist the drainage of Pinchbeck and South Fens. The cost of these engines was £26,000 but increased the usable acreage available by over 25,000 acres. The extensive grazing farms in this part of Lincolnshire supplied Yorkshire manufacturers with great quantities of wool, especially the long wool used by worsted spinners.

With the advent of the railways, freight traffic was quickly taken from inshore boats on the River Welland and the unkempt, boggy roads traversed by pack horses. By 1856 trains were advertised: '. . . . six or seven times a day to all parts, and goods trains daily. The GNR are carriers to all parts and have a parcel office at the White Hart Hotel. Mr Thomas Fellowes is the station master and William Jackson, inspector. An omnibus from the White Hart meets all trains.'

Spalding became a crossing place for three main railway routes. The first was the GN Loop line in 1848. Later lines came east through Holbeach, via the Norwich and Spalding Railway, opening on 15th November, 1858, and west through Bourne opening on 1st August, 1866. These later formed part of the Midland and Great Northern Joint Railway of 1893. In 1867 a line running south-east to March, in Cambridgeshire, arrived in Spalding and in 1882, the Great Northern and Great Eastern Joint Railway ran north-west to Lincoln and on to south Yorkshire. There were also important connections with Grimsby and Hull via the East Lincolnshire Railway.

The station, designed by John Taylor, opened in October 1848, as part of the GNR Lincolnshire Loop. Situated at the west end of the town, the station consisted of two platforms, a small building and a three storey house. It increased in size over the years and was largely rebuilt and resignalled as part of the construction of the GN & GE Joint line. There were two large island platforms, a main line platform and a bay at the north end. At its widest the layout was 18 tracks wide and required five signal boxes to operate it.

The GN & GE Joint line joined the Peterborough to Boston line at Spalding No. 1 signal box, which also dealt with spurs round from the M&GN by which trains gained access to the station, reversing in the process. Through M&GN traffic passed directly east to west, south of the town. No. 2 box controlled traffic to Boston.

Passenger trains through Spalding station were a good mix of stopping trains and express traffic. The GNR Grimsby to Kings Cross services ran cheek by jowl with the cross-country Harwich-Liverpool and Yarmouth-York trains on the March to Lincoln route and the M&GN's Yarmouth-Birmingham service giving a wonderful mix of GNR green, Midland crimson, GER dark blue and the beautiful yellow ochre M&GN engines. Freight traffic produced some interesting motive power, class 'B16' 4-6-0s running from York to March and Immingham 'B1s' and 'Britannias' working the Kings Cross trains in later years. By this time the pre-grouping M&GN engines had been replaced almost exclusively, by Ivatt class '4' 2-6-0's. The Whitemoor Marshalling Yard, in March, gave a boost to rail freight traffic through Spalding after 1928.

Bulb cultivation began in the Fens in about 1880. The railway were quick to capitalise on the potential traffic; flowers left Spalding in the evening, either in

Class 'J6' 0-6-0 No. 64172 waits to leave Spalding station with a passenger train in the 1950s.
Author's Collection

Class '4MT' 2-6-0 No. 43083, built at Darlington in 1951, on an up goods at Spalding on 23rd June, 1954.
Horace Gamble

Ruston and Hornsby-built diesel shunter, Works No. 304469, seen here at Spalding sugar beet factory on 29th June, 1958.   *John R. Bonsor*

Another view of Spalding sugar beet factory, 2nd September, 1967.   *John R. Bonsor*

small loads by passenger trains or on special workings to reach fast passenger or goods services at Peterborough. The Spalding annual flower parade began in 1959 and British Rail exploited its potential by running excursions to the event from many parts of the country for many years. This traffic continues albeit in a much reduced form. A sugar beet factory opened in 1926, access to its sidings being just north of Spalding station. These sidings were also used by Van Geests for the storage of bananas.

Spalding's decline as a railway centre began on 28th February, 1958, when the former M&GN line closed to passengers. The line remained open to freight traffic until 1965. The biggest blow, however, was the closure of the Grimsby to Peterborough route on 3rd October, 1970. Support from Spalding and Holland councils ensured the reopening of the Spalding-Peterborough section on 7th June, 1971. The Harwich boat trains were diverted on 7th May, 1973, bringing to an end main line workings through Spalding. Traffic to the sugar beet factory ceased in 1980 and most of the goods facilities were removed. Trains to March finished on 1st November, 1982. By 1984, all that remained at Spalding were two through lines and a few sidings. The Peterborough service, however, has been well patronised, and a £3 million cash injection for the Peterborough-Doncaster line is in the pipeline.

Surfleet

Modest brick-built station buildings were situated on the down side next to a level crossing with the road serving the nearby village of Surfleet, described in 1856 as 'a well built village near an artificial channel of the River Welland and the small River Glenn, four miles north of Spalding, 945 souls'. The signal box stood on the other side of the crossing, also on the down side. The up side had a small wooden waiting shelter and there were sidings behind both platforms, the one behind the down platform surviving to the end. The station closed to passengers on 11th September, 1961 and for goods traffic on 30th December, 1963.

Algarkirk and Sutterton

This boasted an extensive layout, with sidings on both sides of the track and a goods shed behind the down platform. The signal box was on the up side at the north end of the platform. There were crossings at both ends of the station, the most important being the A17 at the south end.

As well as the usual agricultural produce, prawns and shrimps were loaded into box wagons for early morning sale at Billingsgate Market, in London.

On 2nd April, 1862, the 2.05 am Mail train from Peterborough was derailed while travelling at 40 mph, just after passing Algakirk and Sutterton station. The permanenent way was still that laid 14 years earlier and the wooden trenails had given way allowing the track to spread under the weight of the train. The engine No. 216 and two carriages fell on their side and the brake van was smashed. The driver and guard were both thrown clear and not seriously hurt, the train carried no passengers. The inspecting officer recommended that

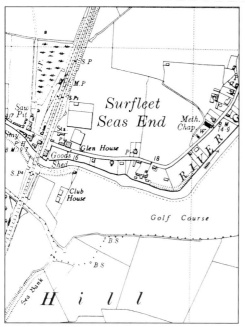

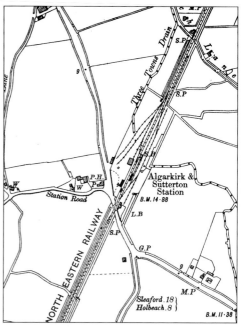

Surfleet station.
Reproduced from Provisional Edition of 6 in. Ordnance Survey map revised 1903 & 1950

Algarkirk & Sutterton station
Reproduced from 1932 edition of 6 in. Ordnance Survey map

Kirton station.
Reproduced from Provisional Edition of 6 in. Ordnance Survey Map revised 1952.

Langrick station.
Reproduced from Provisional Edition of 6 in. Ordnance Survey Map revised 1904 & 1947.

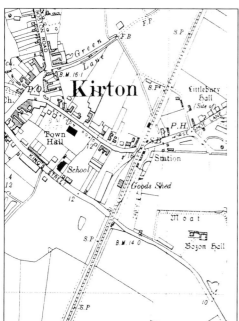

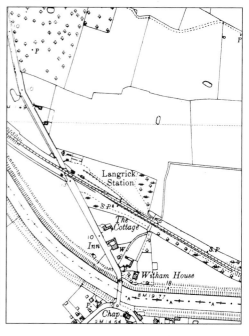

Surfleet station, crossing and signal box on 3rd October, 1959.   *H.B. Priestley*

Surfleet station in the 1960s.   *D. Thompson*

Two class 'B1' 4-6-0 locomotives work a passenger train through Algarkirk and Sutterton station on 6th September, 1957. The pilot engine No. 61264 is one of only two preserved 'B1s' at present based on the Great Central Railway at Loughborough. *H.B. Priestley*

Algarkirk and Sutterton station in 1963 with a locomotive shunting the siding. *D. Thompson*

the chairs should have been secured to the sleepers with iron spikes as well as trenails. It subsequently became practice to manufacture chairs with three holes for the insertion of two trenails and an iron spike.

For the last 20 years or so Algarkirk signal box had no regular men, the level crossing ground frame at the south end of the layout controlled the signals, the box only being switched in when a relief signalman was available, something of a rarity.

Kirton

Kirton was a marshalling place for the potato traffic and had four sidings, and a loading dock on the down side. There was an up siding and an up shunting siding, all controlled from the signal box which stood next to Horse Shoe Lane Crossing. The platforms were staggered either side of this crossing, the up platform being to the south. There was a further level crossing at the southern end of the layout.

As well as potatoes, sugar beet, celery, cattle food and fertilizers were loaded and unloaded at Kirton.

(Sidings at Boston included Calders Yard, dealing with telegraph poles and pit props. The canning firm of Lin Can had a siding with access into the factory. The Boston Dock line ran across a main road, over the river, via a railway owned swing bridge, to the dock sidings. Here was a coal hoist for the export of coal, also a grain silo and warehouses for imported fruit and vegetables. British Rail had two shifts of shunters, loaders and sheeters employed on the dock.)

Hall Hills

The GNR bought Bethell & Company's Hall Hills creosoting plant for £5,000 in May 1887. Railway sleepers were made from Baltic timber, imported through the port of Immingham and moved forward by train loads to Hall Hills for pressure creosoting. The plant occupied an area of 23 acres and was sited on part of the old river bed.

Until just after World War II, nearly all the timber used for the manufacture of sleepers had been obtained from the Baltic. The trees used were Baltic Redwood. A similar type of timber was also grown in Scotland and also used for sleepers.

In the years between the two World Wars, Oregon Pine and Douglas Fir was increasingly imported from America and Canada. During World War II this timber was relied upon almost exclusively.

In the case of Baltic timbers the immense forests of Russia and Poland produced slow growing, hard, resinous timber, considered ready for felling after about 50 years of growth. They were logged in the forests to dimensions of 10 ft x 10 ft or 10 ft x 5 ft and cross sawn to approximately 8 ft 6 in. lengths, after which they were floated to the Baltic and White Sea ports by a system of lakes and waterways for shipment to Britain. On arrival the 10 ft x 5 ft pieces

Brush type '2' A1A-A1A No. D5614 with a passenger train near Algarkirk and Sutterton on Sunday 19th June, 1960. *Andrew C. Ingram Collection*

A 1963 view of Kirton station showing the staggered platforms either side of the level crossing, a feature of many east Lincolnshire stations. *D. Thompson*

A nice shot of the elegant signal box at Kirton in August 1970.

P. Grey

Langrick station in 1963; note the 'British Railways' tender parked behind the station which contained the station's water supply.
D. Thompson

The station house at Langrick in 1963.
D. Thompson

were conveyed direct to the railway creosoting depots, the 10 ft x 10 ft pieces were discharged into water, to be sawn down the middle at sawmills, before despatch. The sleepers reached maturity by seasoning in the depots, after which they were bored for fastenings and creosoted under pressure, before the chairs were affixed.

For creosoting the sleepers were passed on trucks into large cylinders some 6 ft in diameter. The creosote was inserted under a pressure of approximately 180 lb. per square inch, at a temperature of 185 degrees Fahrenheit. The time in the cylinder may have been as long as 3 hours, depending on the nature of the timber. Baltic timber absorbed nearly 3 gallons of creosote, as compared with 1½ gallons in the case of Douglas Fir. Partly because Douglas Fir and hardwood sleepers did not absorb creosote as well as Baltic timber, their life on the track was shorter - about 17 years with no residual value, whilst the Baltic timbers lasted 25 years in the running lines and had a further usage in sidings and for roads and fencing.

The plant at Hall Hills had extensive sidings of both standard and narrow gauge, the latter running inside the former*. Hall Hills signal box worked 2 shifts and controlled access to the plant. The box, with a 25 lever Mackenzie & Holland frame, opened in 1902. A disastrous fire destroyed the creosote plant building and pump house, together with sleepers, timbers and wagons, on 14th April, 1957. However the plant and the box continued to operate until 10th January, 1965, when the short spur then remaining to the depot was closed.

Langrick

Situated five miles north-west of Boston, Langrick station had a similar layout to Dogdyke, although more accessible, with a road crossing at the west end of the station. The usual GNR three storey tower was here replaced by a strange little pantiled belfry. This was a large building and stood at right angles to the up platform. A large wooden goods shed stood in the goods yard to the east and behind the up platform. The station master lived in a more recent house, the original rooms near the station being taken over as traffic increased on the line. The station was closed for passenger and goods on 17th June, 1967.

Langrick signal box was worked on three shifts. Percy Carter recalled an annual regatta on the River Witham, at Antons Gowt, situated between Hall Hills and Langrick: 'All the boats had to be carried across the railway at a curved section of the line. There was a telephone communication between there and Langrick box. Myself and a police officer were in charge of the operation on several occasions. Boats which had taken part in the Oxford and Cambridge boat race took part, so the event was of some importance'.

Dogdyke

A township of scattered houses in Billinghay parish, two miles south-south-west of Tattershall, on the west bank of the Witham, extending southward from a bridge on the Sleaford road.

The station had a similar layout to Langrick although less symetrical. The

* See Motive Power chapter.

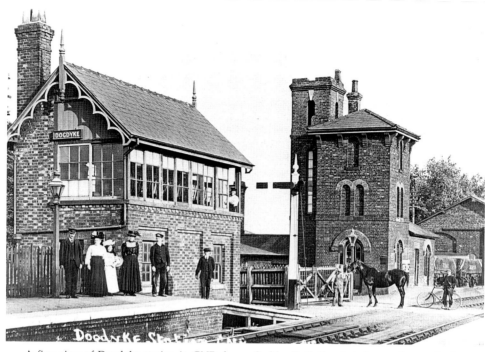

A fine view of Dogdyke station in GNR days. Goddard's Italianate influence is seen in the design of the buildings which were built by Stephen Dawson in 1849. *D.N. Robinson Collection*

A compact view of Dogdyke station on 18th May, 1959, apart from the station master's house and the platform railings, none of this remains today. *H.B. Priestley*

The curved platforms of Dogdyke station seen here in 1963. Sinclair's siding and warehouse are behind the platform.   *D. Thompson*

Fisherman wait to catch the 3.51 pm Boston to Doncaster train at Dogdyke on 22nd October, 1961. Class 'B1' 4-6-0 No. 61282 is the train engine.   *John Porter Collection*

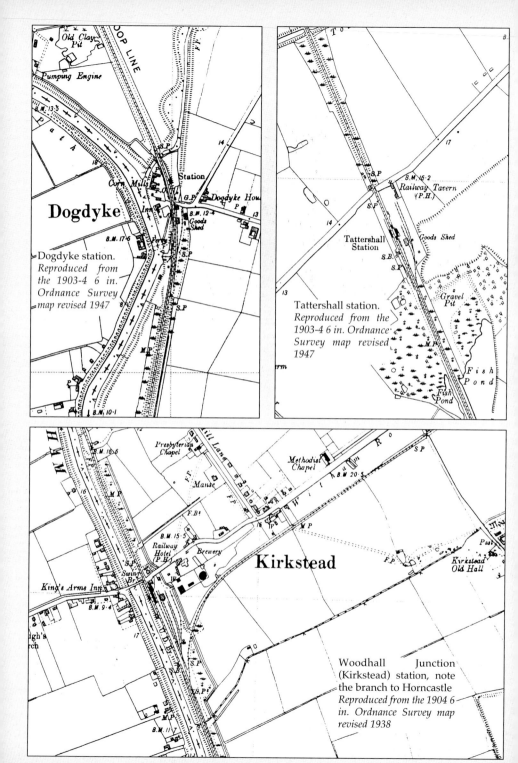

Dogdyke station.
Reproduced from the 1903-4 6 in. Ordnance Survey map revised 1947

Tattershall station.
Reproduced from the 1903-4 6 in. Ordnance Survey map revised 1947

Woodhall Junction (Kirkstead) station, note the branch to Horncastle
Reproduced from the 1904 6 in. Ordnance Survey map revised 1938

A passenger train at Tattershall station. Locomotive No. 4 was a Stirling 2-2-2, built in 1868. The train is travelling to Boston.

Author's Collection

Tattershall station looking towards Boston in 1963.

D. Thompson

The Italianate style buildings at Tattershall in June 1956, this style was a feature of stations on the Loop Line.

H.B. Priestley

station area was very narrow, the various buildings divided by a road crossing, giving access to the ferry and the 'Packet Inn'. In 1856 the Inn was run by James Sampson, who also operated the ferry. To the north of the road crossing were the station platforms, wooden waiting rooms, signal box and siding to Sinclair's warehouse and corn mill. The station master's house of Italianate design, goods shed and sidings and railway cottages were situated to the south of the crossing. The station signal box was operated on two shifts; one of the signalmen lived in a railway cottage and looked after the gates at night when the box was closed. The station buildings were burnt down in 1965.

A wind powered pumping engine at Dogdyke was used to drain the surrounding land. Wind power was replaced by a beam engine in 1856, this engine still survives as part of the Dogdyke Steam Pumping Engine Preservation Trust. Eels, caught by the attendant of the pumping station, were packed in crates and sent to London from Dogdyke station. It was reckoned that he earned more from this trade than from his full-time job at the pumping station.

Sinclair's siding served a mill and coal yard; the firm had a solid tyred Model 'T' Ford lorry, which was used to run between the siding and their headquarters in the nearby village of New York.

Mr Grainger, who ran Holmes Stores, in New York, cycled to Dogdyke station each Wednesday morning to catch the 8 o'clock train to Boston. He would travel with a Gladstone bag chained to his wrist. In Boston he would purchase goods for the New York shop, bringing lighter portable goods back with him. The rest of the goods would be collected by young Bert Eyre on Thursday.

Bert started working at the shop when he was fourteen; one of his duties was to go to Dogdyke station to collect the weekly local and national papers and magazines. These would be sorted out at the station and some of the deliveries made along the route back to the shop. The papers had to be signed for at the station. At that time Bert was learning italic handwriting, and on his visit to collect the papers his signature was refused because 'it wasn't joined up writing'.

The stores later bought a Model 'T' Ford lorry, which was used for fetching and carrying and delivering. Items such as vinegar and paraffin and general groceries would be delivered and eggs and butter bought in for the shop. The lorry also collected a five ton load of salt from the station, which was used for salting meat in the days before refrigeration.

Tattershall

Celebrated for the remains of its ancient, beautiful, castle, Tattershall was described in White's Directory of 1856 as, 'a small market town on a plain on the west side of the River Witham, and having 650 inhabitants. The remains of the castle, built in 1400, offer the best specimens of ancient brickwork still in existence. The station is situated about 3/4 mile south-west of the town'.

Tattershall signal box, along with those at Langrick, Dogdyke and Woodhall Junction, was operated by what was known as a horse rake frame, not the normal straight-up lever frames. At one time the GNR were discussing the possibility of using these frames in all future signalling schemes. They were being removed from Lincolnshire boxes during the 1950s. A further point of interest concerned the crossover points leading from the up to the down main or vice versa; these were operated by two levers Nos. 22½ and 23½. Tattershall station crossing, which crossed the A153 road, was operated in a very antiquated way. When the signal box was closed the gatekeeper had indicators to show the positions of up and down trains. The signals were connected to separate wires which worked as follows: as soon as the gateman started to open the gates the signals began to lower. They were not fully off until the gates were in the correct position for the passage of the train.

Beet, potatoes, corn and wool were loaded here. Sacks were hired from the railway company for various farm products, the weight of the sack being determined by its contents: 19 stones of beans or peas, 18 stones of wheat, 16 stones of barley and 12 stones of oats. These would be manhandled. Fleeces were made into 'bales' or 'sheets', stitched together with heavy wooden pegs, the work done on the farm. Each 'sheet' held 40 fleeces and was hauled onto farm wagons by the use of wooden planks. Unloading took place in Tattershall goods shed*.

Sheep, pigs and cattle were loaded, and occasionally off-loaded at the station. Ray Goose, whose grandfather and father ran the village butcher's shop before him, recalled cycling with his brother to Tattershall station in the mid 1930s,

. . . . to collect animals purchased previously at Boston Livestock market. The journey from the station to the slaughterhouse was often difficult, the animals wandering into fields and gardens if not watched carefully. After this time road transport began to take over the farm-to-market-to-slaughterhouse transportation of livestock.

Around this time there were three or four poultry packers in the area, who travelled around in what was the forerunner of the present day pick-up truck, with wooden crates on the back. During the morning they would buy live poultry, later in the day they would kill, pluck and dress the birds and despatch them by rail from Tattershall to Smithfield Market, in London.

Up to World War II we used to grow a few acres of early potatoes which we would pack in wooden barrels. These were collected later the same day by the local railway lorry and put on rail for Bradford Market.

For years Farmer Porter, of Tattershall had been trying to get the railway company to define and enclose the boundary alongside the old ballast pits near the station, with no success. One summer day he decided to let his sheep graze in the old pits, from where they wandered onto the railway, causing some inconvenience. The outcome was the almost immediate erection of a fence by the railway company.

Marsh Lane Crossing gates were opened and closed by farm users. A bell would ring at the crossing, operated by the train striking a treadle between the rails as it approached the crossing. There was another treadle on the crossing which would stop the bell ringing, unless a train was approaching from the other direction. J. Sawyer, a seed salesman, was killed on the crossing by a Boston-Lincoln train in 1959 when his car was hit by the train.

* A few years ago the author helped Alan Turner of the Lincolnshire Railway Museum to remove the wooden jibbed crane from the goods shed at Tattershall and into safe keeping of the museum.

An extremely interesting view of Kirkstead station in the 1880s, with river and rail traffic in evidence. The ferry across the Witham closed in 1891 when the GNR repalced it with swing bridge.
D.N. Robinson Collection

A very neat Woodhall Junction station with extremely well kept gardens, seen here in 1924. The Horncastle bay is to the right.
Horace Neale

Coningsby Junction opened on 1st June, 1913 to allow access to the Kirkstead-Little Steeping Railway (The New Line). The junction was in a very isolated spot, over a mile from the nearest road, 1½ miles south of Kirkstead station.

Woodhall Junction (Kirkstead)

The station buildings of 1848 were added to in 1855 for the opening of the Horncastle branch line. As the junction was situated south of the station, a bay was built for branch trains from which they reversed to gain the junction, before going forward onto the branch. The original name, Kirkstead, was changed to Woodhall Junction on 10th July, 1922.

The Italianate-style station house building, with its tall, narrow, three storey tower, had a particularly large chimney block and overhanging roof; the windows had semi-circular arches. It has been suggested that these three storey towers were used for flag signalling in the early days of the line. This Italianate style was characteristic of many of the station houses on the line. Similar buildings were to be found at Peakirk, Spalding and Tattershall, although there were differences. Yellow bricks predominated at all stations except Woodhall Junction where they were used to provide a decorative alternative to the red brick of the building. A similar roof arrangement, with huge ornate chimneys rising over the chamfered roofs, existed at Bardney. A large canopy, supported on wooden pillars, was provided on the platform for Boston, also serving the bay. On the down side a small canopy was attached to the waiting shelter, next to which stood an ornate cast-iron gents' urinal, now preserved at the Museum of Lincolnshire Life, in Lincoln. At one time a large square water tank stood atop a brick base between the platform end and the signal box, which was on the down side of the track south of the station. There was a level crossing to the north of the station. The gates were operated by gatemen acting upon bell codes received from the signal box. When a ferry crossed the Witham at Woodhall Junction (up until 1960), the gatemen lived in two cottages nearby and took toll money from ferry passengers. Woodhall Junction box was worked on three shifts.

An Engineering Department motor trolley was kept here, and at Langrick, used for conveying men and materials to any required point during track maintenance. Engineer gangers were Messrs Gray and Howard and patrolmen, White and Townell.

Stixwould

An ancient village overlooking the vale of the Witham with 225 inhabitants (1856). The layout here was similar to that at Southrey except for a slight difference in the arrangement of the platform shelters. The platforms were rebuilt by the LNER with standard components. A two storey station house stood at right angles to the track, gable-ended with decorative bargeboards, and with upper floor windows also gabled. Other facilities were single storey station buildings and a signal box and goods yard. Drinking water and paraffin for the station was brought in by train.

Top: Clayton steam railcar, *Bang Up* seen at Woodhall Junction station during running trials in 1928. *Bang Up* could accommodate 64 passengers and was one of 11 railcars built by the Clayton Wagon Company for the LNER. *Author's Collection*

Centre: A nice view of Woodhall Junction station on 29th April, 1954 showing the splendid station nameboard and the now preserved, cast-iron gents' urinal next to the station waiting shelter. Class 'B1' No. 61281 is seen here with the 9.00 am Lincoln-Skegness train.

R.M. Casserley

Bottom: Woodhall Junction station looking towards Lincoln and showing the new flyover in place, note the cycle rack on the up platform. *Author's Collection*

The splendid signal box at Stixwould with an, unfortunately, unknown signalman, in August 1970. *P. Grey*

A fine view of Stixwould station taken just before closure in 1970. It represents a scene little changed over the 122 years of its active life. *P. Grey*

Southrey station in August 1970 showing the GNR concrete station nameboards. *P. Grey*

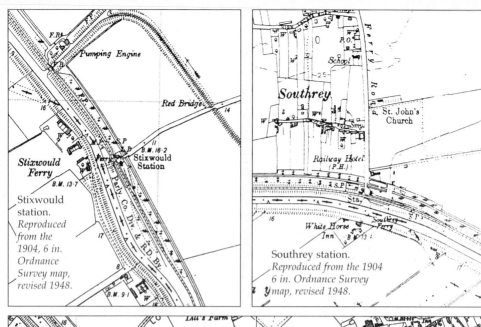

Stixwould
station.
*Reproduced
from the
1904, 6 in.
Ordnance
Survey map,
revised 1948.*

Southrey station.
*Reproduced from the 1904
6 in. Ordnance Survey
map, revised 1948.*

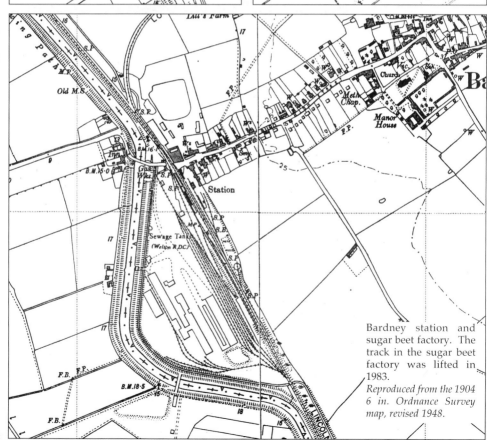

Bardney station and
sugar beet factory. The
track in the sugar beet
factory was lifted in
1983.
*Reproduced from the 1904
6 in. Ordnance Survey
map, revised 1948.*

When the station lost its station master and came under the authority of the station master at Woodhall Junction, the station house was occupied by the signalman and his wife who operated the ferry, which was capable of carrying motor vehicles, and sold food and cigarettes to the fishermen. The signal box was operated for one shift, 11.30 am to 9.30 pm.

The goods yard closed on 17th June, 1963.

Southrey

The village of Southrey is situated in the parish of Bardney and was descibed as 'a quaint little village with about 60 houses and a population of 200'. Southrey kept its ferry for some time after others had been replaced by bridges, charging 2d. per person, 3d. for cycles.

The station house at Southrey was set at right angles to the track, and the layout was, in all respects, similar to Stixwould. Unlike Stixwould, however, the platforms at Southrey retained their vertical brick walled faces with diamond pattern edging. The station was under the authority of the station master at Bardney.

The signal box was operated by a signalman and a porter/signalman, both of whom carried out booking office duties. Percy Carter remembers moving to Southrey station in January 1937. 'We moved house from a cottage at Marsh Lane to the station house at Southrey. Our furniture should have been taken to Southrey station from Tattershall by a goods train from Boston. However, owing to a derailment at Langrick, this train was cancelled and we finished up sleeping on the floor for our first night at Southrey'. The goods yard closed on 1st October, 1955.

Bardney

Prior to the opening of the Louth and Lincoln Railway in 1876, Bardney had an up and down platform, station buildings with an 'Italianate' house, a goods shed and sidings.

The Louth and Lincoln Railway was incorporated on 6th August, 1866; the original intention being to join the GNR Loop at Five Mile House with a junction facing Lincoln. However land purchase problems prevented this and when the branch opened it joined the Loop at Bardney station with a junction facing the wrong way for trains to Lincoln. Prior to the branch opening, Captain Tyler inspected the line, suggesting alterations at Bardney. By the time of his second inspection the GNR had authorised the expenditure of £4,500 to meet his requirements, including a new signal box and a double line junction. In July 1877 a further alteration to the layout and a new platform was completed. The final arrangement was of three platform faces, two of which formed an island with a canopied waiting shelter, the third was a short platform used by the Louth trains. The waiting room on the island platform was demolished in 1967.

A second signal box was opened at Bardney, in conjunction with the opening of the Louth line. The boxes were known as Bardney North and Bardney South,

Bardney station looking towards Boston. Main line services used the island platform, the short platform in front of the station buildings was used by trains for Louth via Wragby and Donington-on-Bain. The line running off to the right behind the water column was the return line from the sugar factory sidings.　　　　　　　　　　　　　　　　　　*D. Thompson*

Bardney station in its final years.　　　　　　　　　　　　　　*Robert Humm Collection*

LNER class 'D2' 4-4-0 with a local train passing the sugar factory and approaching Bardney station, notice the GNR somersault signal. *N.E. Stead*

Class 'A5' 4-6-2T No. 69804 shunts at Bardney on 28th April, 1954. *H.C. Casserley*

Five Mile House signal box alongside the River Witham. The ferry is being used as a makeshift diving board on a hot summer day.

E. Steele

Bardney signal box two months before closure, the building alongside it is Morrells canning factory which was served by a private siding.

P. Grey

the latter also known as 'station' box. The North box was situated just beyond of the level crossing at the north end of the station. South box was sited east of the platforms and adjacent to the goods yard. The North box worked the South box down and up home signals during the time the latter box was closed. After the South box closed, in 1924, North box assumed the title Station box, and received a new frame along the back wall. Bardney was a three shift box, dealing with traffic on the Loop, as well as trains to and from Louth and the Sugar Factory and Morrells siding (*see Appendices 2 and 3*).

Five Mile House

The station was named after a public house, which was a bargee inn, used especially by horse-drawn packets. The pub building became part of the station which only lasted until the end of 1850, when it was closed because of lack of traffic. It reopened in 1865 when a local farmer requested siding facilities, which was granted. This was a short siding capable of holding about a dozen wagons. Freight traffic was never particularly heavy, the main loads being potatoes, grain and odd loads of hay and sugar beet. In the early 1920s Fred Andrew, a farmer from Ferry Hill, brought beet to be transported to Kelham Factory, at Newark, (prior to the Bardney factory opening). Fred had to move his beet 2 miles to the station by horse drawn wagon, as his farm was on the Fiskerton side of the river this also meant using the ferry. This kind of difficult journey deterred a good many potential railway customers. One man, named Hyde, however, acquired a barge to carry his produce from Branston Island the two miles to the station, by water, hauled by horse. The load comprised baled hay for despatch by rail and fertilizer for the return trip. The hay was duly forwarded and then the fertilizer loaded onto the barge. The only problem was the heaviness of the fertilizer which, combined with the shallowness of the water conspired to render the barge firmly grounded. This required some off-loading and two trips to Branston Island. Mr Hyde and his barge were not seen again at the station.

Norman Clark described market day events at the station.

We expected 20 or 30 passengers for the 10.15 am (Fridays) to Lincoln. Farmer Smith arrived by bicycle, which he left unlocked against the station fence. He bought his 10*d*. return ticket, taking with him a sample of his corn in his pocket. At the corn exchange he would do a deal with a merchant and hands were shaken. Eventually a transfer note from merchant 'A' was received by the station master, as follows: 'You will receive 20 quarters of wheat from Mr Smith, please transfer to the order of Messrs 'B' & Co'. Later another note, from Messrs 'B' & Co.' 'You will receive 20 quarters of wheat from Messrs 'A' & Co., please transfer to the order of Messrs 'C' & Co. The corn was passing (on paper) from one merchant to another, each getting a nice little rake off for the transaction; in the meantime Farmer Smith was the victim, waiting for the station master to tell him that the forwarding order had been received. When it did arrive, from Messrs 'C' & Co., for instance, it read, 'You will receive 20 quarters of wheat. Please forward to Messrs Dickinson, the miller at Lincoln'. The consignment was 'railed' and sent 5 miles to Lincoln; Farmer Smith was left to pick up the bill for demurrage and the hire of the railway sacks.

This photograph gives a sense of the isolated location of Five Mile House station. Class 'K3' 2-6-0 No. 61896 is seen at the station with a Skegness excursion on 16th July, 1950.

P.H. Wells

Class 'A1/1' 4-6-2 No. 60113 *Great Northern* heads the down 'Centenary Special' through Five Mile House station on 6th July, 1950. The portrait on the smokebox door is of Edmund Denison and the trip ran from Kings Cross to York. *P.H. Wells*

Washingborough station in GNR days showing its proximity to the river. *Author's Collection*

Washingborough station looking south, GNR days. *D.N. Robinson Collection*

Washingborough Junction, the River Witham on the right and Lincoln Cathedral in the distance. The line following the course of the river is the Loop Line. A passenger train moves off the Washingborough-Greetwell Junction section of the Lincoln Avoiding line onto the Loop whilst a goods train waits its turn.

George Flatters

Washingborough Junction looking south on 25th June, 1955. Annesley based class 'K3' 2-6-0 No. 61856, with a seaside excursion train, passes an elegant GNR lattice somersault signal.

George Flatters

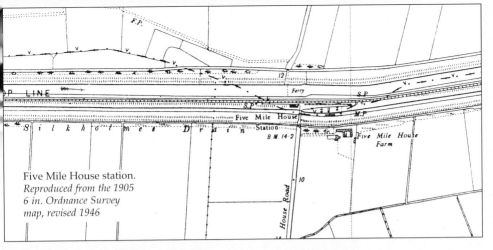

Five Mile House station.
*Reproduced from the 1905
6 in. Ordnance Survey
map, revised 1946*

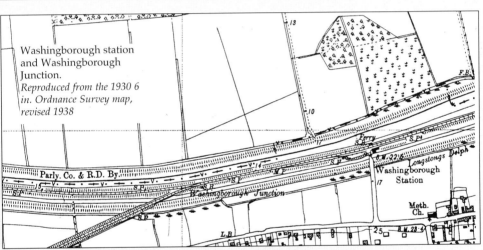

Washingborough station
and Washingborough
Junction.
*Reproduced from the 1930 6
in. Ordnance Survey map,
revised 1938*

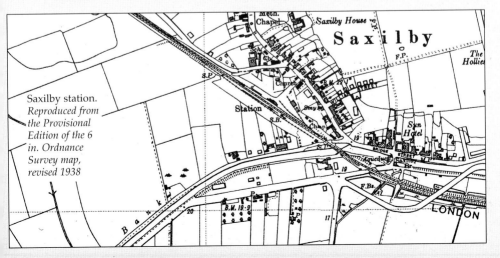

Saxilby station.
*Reproduced from
the Provisional
Edition of the 6
in. Ordnance
Survey map,
revised 1938*

George Capes was station master until the fire in 1919 (*see Chapter 2*). George Ripley took over, lodging nearby. Two small buildings, one used as an office, the other as a waiting room, replaced the destroyed station buildings; the signal box was rebuilt. The station closed on 27th July, 1940, and the buildings were destroyed by fire in early 1960.

Washingborough

A desolate spot which, unsurprisingly, was the first station on the line to lose both passenger and goods services, on 29th July, 1940. The station buildings comprised a single storey brick built structure on the up platform, end on to which was a flat-roofed shelter joining it to a substantial residence, standing at right angles to the line. The signal box stood directly opposite, alongside a crossing which allowed access to and from the ferry. The station box up starting signal was worked by the box at Washingborough Junction during the time the former was closed.

Beyond Washingborough station the line passed Washingborough Junction, connecting it with the GN & GEJR Lincoln avoiding line, and on past Sincil Bank and Pelham Street Junction signal boxes on the down side, before entering Lincoln Central station. Running over High Street crossing, East and West Holmes boxes were on the up side, before the line arrived at Pyewipe Junction, at which point the LD&ECR joined the Loop.

The GNR served the engineering firm of Robey and Co. Ltd and Clarke's Crank and Forge Co. Ltd in Lincoln. Newsum's were connected to the GN by West Holmes signal box, the siding crossing the Fossdyke by a drawbridge.

Saxilby

Saxilby was described in 1856 as, 'A large, well-built, imposing village on the north side of the Fossdyke, six miles north-west by west of Lincoln, and twelve miles south-south-east of Gainsborough. The station situated on the south side of the village. Market products to Lincoln every Friday courtesy of William Leverton'.

The railway ran north-west with the Fossdyke on its right, passing Rowlands Siding signal box, which was situated 1,397 yards beyond Pyewipe Junction, on the up side. The box served a small basin for barges with a single line off to the left. Next came Kesteven Siding on the right, at which point the distance between the railway and the canal widened sufficiently to allow the construction of a chemical fertilizer factory.

At Saxilby the line crossed the canal and ran over a roadway to enter the station. The main building was constructed of brick and situated on the up side; behind this platform ran a long down refuge siding. The goods shed and yard was also situated on the up side. The signal box was at the southern end of the down platform until 1922, when it was moved to the level crossing at the south-east end of the layout, this time on the up side. With the provision of an up loop to the north much lever pulling was involved, spring points and a ground frame controlling entry to the siding. Instructions for use were as follows:

Plenty of railway staff in this late 19th century view of Saxilby station, by this time under GN&GE Joint jurisdiction.
Author's Collection

The crossing keeper's cottage at Saxilby station in the early 1900s.
Lincolnshire Libraries

Saxilby station looking south on 3rd May, 1975, the modern lights intruding on a timeless scene.
N.D. Mundy

British Railways class '5' No. 73162 heading north with a passenger train crosses the Fossdyke at Saxilby.
Peter Washbourne

Down Refuge Siding. This siding is controlled by a ground frame locked from the signal box. When on duty the station staff will operate the ground levers, at other times the guard will be responsible for this duty. In all cases the guard must ride in the brake van while the train is setting back into the siding. Immediately the train is clear in the siding the fireman must put back the ground levers. After the train has come to a stand in the siding, the guard must go to the ground frame and be prepared to work the levers when unlocked by the signalman for the train to leave the siding, rejoining his train after it has drawn clear on to the running line and he has closed the siding points. The signalman must allow the guard time to carry out his duty before lowering the down advance signal.

Sykes Junction, 1½ miles beyond Saxilby belonged to the GCR serving its line to Retford and controlled by a signal box on a low embankment on the down side. A small signal box at Sturton, between Sykes Junction and Stow Park appeared to serve no other purpose than to divide up the block section.

Stow Park

The station was situated just south of a level crossing with a Roman road running east-west towards the village of Marton. The station was called 'Marton' until 1st December, 1871, at which time it became, 'Stow Park for Marton', in order to distinguish it from Marton on the North Eastern Railway.

The station lay a mile from Marton and two miles from the village of Stow. The station buildings stood opposite the signal box at the level crossing, the goods shed and yard were behind the up side platform. A down lay-by siding was at the south of the layout.

Lea

The station building and four cottages were at the level of a road, to the west of an overbridge. The platforms and waiting shelters were in a cutting approached from the road by a flight of stairs. During the revamping of the Lincoln to Gainsborough section, in 1864, the formation at Lea was lowered by some 20 ft, sinking the platforms into a cutting and leaving the station buildings high up at road level.

An approach led to the goods yard on the up side. The signal box and refuge siding were opposite. The villages of Lee and Knaith were a good two miles distance from the station.

An accident was reported in 1860, concerning a passenger train which left Gainsborough bound for Lincoln at 4.30 pm. The train had proceeded to within about ½ a mile of Lea station when it came into collision with some object with such violence as to throw most of the passengers out of their seats. The general impression was that the train had run off the rails. After a time the engine was brought to a standstill and, on examination, a heifer was found under the engine 'mashed into mummy', according to an eyewitness.

A neat looking Stow Park station seen here in 1963.   *D. Thompson*

Stow Park signal box and goods shed in 1987.   *Andrew C. Ingram Collection*

Lea station taken from the road bridge and looking towards Stow Park in the 1930s.

D.N. Robinson Collection

Lea station looking towards Gainsborough. The far arched bridge carried the B1241 over the line, the nearest bridge served a minor road. Note the steps leading from the station buildings to the platforms which were set in a cutting.

D. Thompson

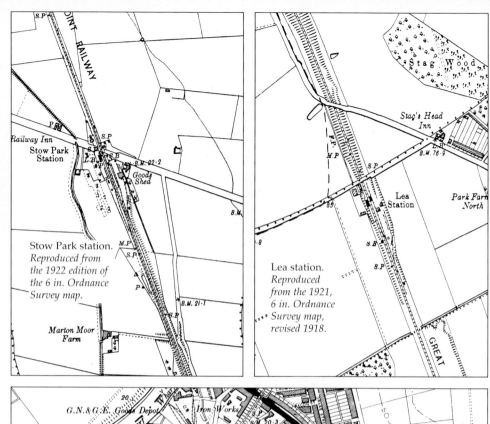

Stow Park station.
*Reproduced from
the 1922 edition of
the 6 in. Ordnance
Survey map.*

Lea station.
*Reproduced
from the 1921,
6 in. Ordnance
Survey map,
revised 1918.*

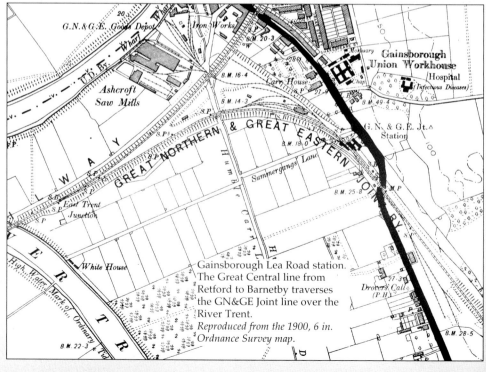

Gainsborough Lea Road station.
The Great Central line from
Retford to Barnetby traverses
the GN&GE Joint line over the
River Trent.
*Reproduced from the 1900, 6 in.
Ordnance Survey map.*

Gainsborough

Gainsborough, situated on the River Trent, was accessible to sea-going vessels. In the 1700s the town flourished as goods were transferred between the sea-going and the river-going vessels. A considerable trade was carried on and Staffordshire, Leicestershire, Nottinghamshire and parts of Lincolnshire were supplied with goods from London and the north through the port. By 1834, 158,000 tons of goods and merchandise were annually transhipped, 30, 000 tons of coal, lime and stone arrived in the town and 50,000 tons passed through by river. On 6th January, 1841 the Port of Gainsborough was opened for exportation and importation and bonding of foreign goods. This success was, however, cut short by the advent of the railways. Customs and Excise duties fell from £73,231, in 1844 to a mere £13,224 by 1854.

At this time a considerable trade with the Baltic was carried out; the town had extensive mills for crushing linseed, three breweries, several large malt kilns, timber yards, three ship yards and a dry dock. Steam packets still worked from Gainsborough to Hull and Newcastle-on-Tyne, twice a week. There was much traffic in corn, timber and linseed and great quantities of gypsum was quarried in the area and sent to various parts of the country for plastering and agricultural purposes.

Gainsborough began to decline after the opening of the MS&LR and the docks at Grimsby. However the growth of Marshall's engineering works accelerated by 1870, bringing a new kind of prosperity to the town.

Between Lea and the station at Lea Road, Gainsborough, the Loop line passed Sir Charles Anderson's siding and Ballast Road siding, crossing over the A156 road by means of a skew bridge, to enter Lea Road station. The station, situated on an embankment and a curve was located about ¾ mile from the town centre. The Italianate-style station buildings were reached from the staggered platforms by two flights of steps contained within a fine wooden covered stairway.

A top goods yard, with a goods shed and cattle pens, was located on the outside of the curve. A long branch trailed down beneath the MS&LR line from Gainsborough Central station, to reach the lower yard, with its GN & GEJR goods depot on the Trent, the Ashcroft Oil Mills and the Steam Saw and Planing Mills.

Originally a single signal box controlled activities, from a position inside the station curve. This became North box when a South box was provided on the up platform, controlling additional sidings at the south end. South box was the one that survived to become 'Gainsborough Lea Road'. The station was shunted by a Retford based class 'Y3', No. 55, if this was not available a class 'N5' deputised.

Now part of the Lincoln-Doncaster line, Lea Road station has fared much better than its more grandiose MS&LR counterpart. North of the station the goods yard deals mainly with rail oil tankers. Crude oil extracted from many wells around Gainsborough is pumped by landlines to Lea Road. Two or three trainloads leave weekly for a refinery at Llandarcy.

Gainsborough Lea Road station, showing the curved wooden platform. Both of Gainsborough's stations are still open but Lea Road has fared the better of the two. *D.N. Robinson Collection*

Gainsborough Lea Road station from the up platform in May 1975. *N.D. Mundy*

A view of Gainsborough Lea Road station looking across to the buildings on the up platform.

Robert Humm Collection

Gainsborough Lea Road signal box on 6th June, 1969. This box was originally South Box, provided to control additional sidings at the south end of the station. *H.C. Casserley*

GNR 'No. 6' class 7 ft 2-2-2 No. 14 seen here during a cleaning session at Lincoln in 1902,. These engines had a long and useful life on secondary routes after their main line exploits were over. Built in 1868 No. 14 is seen with a Stirling straight back boiler   *LCGB/Ken Nunn Collection*

7 ft 2-2-2 No. 39 as running in 1894. This engine was shedded at Boston in November 1905 and withdrawn in June 1906.   *K.H. Leech Collection*

Chapter Ten

Motive Power

The first engine sheds on the GNR were temporary wooden stuctures, erected as the construction of the line progressed, Boston and Peterborough had such buildings. A similar building was erected at Lincoln, in 1849, but was removed to Gainsborough in 1850; this was a very short lived arrangement, Gainsborough disappearing off the list of active sheds within a year.

At the beginning of May 1848, seven engines and tenders were at the temporary shed at Walton Junction, Peterborough, this effectively being the first GNR engine shed. Made of wood, it remained in place until moved to Boston for the accommodation of carriage repairs, in March 1851. By 29th August, 1848, ten passenger and five goods engines, were at Peterborough, with a further goods engine on loan to the contractors, Peto and Betts.

The permanent engine shed at Peterborough was built by the contractors F.W. Costar. The new shed was an eight road, brick-built structure, with a raised smoke vent running almost the full length of the ridge. At that time accommodation was provided for about 16 engines. Along the east side a 60 ft by 20 ft workshop was provided and offices connected the engine shed with a repair workshop, at the rear of which stood the Great Northern Hotel. A 40 ft turntable was provided and a simple coal stage, with a 23,000 gallon water tank astride its northern end. Peterborough station shed housed all the earlier types of GNR engines during its lifetime. The shed buildings were finally demolished in about 1963 and the turntable removed in 1965.

The GNR's locomotive headquarters were established at Boston in the early days. Construction did not begin until the summer of 1848, and slow progress was a source of some annoyance to the GNR Board. A temporary wooden building was erected, possibly near the station. It is uncertain when Boston works were first occupied although the GNR Board was told, in August 1850, that the engine shed was ready for use. By 1849 there were 39 engines working on the Loop from Boston. Many engines had been housed temporarily at Grimsby or Lincoln, until facilities at Boston became available.

The GNR's locomotive engineer, Edward Bury, set up his offices in Boston, in February 1848. Bury was eventually replaced by Archibald Sturrock, who took up his position in Boston in April 1850.

By June of that year, however, the GNR Board had instructed Sturrock, William and Joseph Cubitt and Seymour Clarke, the General Manager, to find an alternative, and more appropriate, site for the works. The first choice was Peterborough, Sturrock suggesting in a memo of 13th July, 1850 that 'immediate steps should be taken to erect as quickly as possible works at Peterborough sufficient to enable the Locomotive Department to be at once removed thither'.

Certainly enough land was purchased at Peterborough to enable New England yards to be laid out. However in June 1851, the Board decided that the works should be moved to Doncaster. No doubt the influence of Edmund Denison, a prominent Doncaster man, had some bearing on the decision.

135

'392' series 0-6-0ST No. 167 at Lincoln on 4th August, 1902. No. 167 was built in 1873 and
withdrawn in 1904.   *LCGB/Ken Nunn Collection*

'400' class 0-6-0 No. 448 at Lincoln in 1902. Built for the GNR by Neilson & Sons in 1866, No.
448 was used originally for working heavy coal trains. Shown here rebuilt with a Stirling boiler
the engine still retains its original outside frames.   *LCGB/Ken Nunn Collection*

Things moved slowly, and it was not until March 1852 that a tender was accepted for the construction of the new works. About 300 men moved from Boston to Doncaster when the works opened; by the end of 1853, 949 men were employed there.

Boston shed remained active and like many others, was virtually rebuilt after Nationalisation as a nine-road modern structure, which lasted until January 1964.

The wooden building moved from Lincoln to Gainsborough in 1850 was replaced at Lincoln in 1850-51 by a new gable roofed brick-built engine shed. This in turn was replaced when Kirk and Parry erected a shed with two hip roofs, each covering two tracks, on the Holmes in 1875. Like Boston, Lincoln shed was largely rebuilt after Nationalisation. The official closing date was October 1964, although the enginemen's office continued for some time as a booking-on point, with a running foreman in charge.

The GNR installed a 23 ft turntable and watering points at Spalding. By December 1865, the General Manager noted that a larger supply of water would soon be required to be available at Spalding.

A two-road engine shed was built by the Midland Railway in the late 1860s. The 50 ft by 30 ft building was brick-built, with arched entrances at each end and a slated, gabled roof. Although built by the Midland, the maintenance of the building was the responsibility of the GNR, who also paid water and gas dues and maintained the turntable. The original turntable was replaced by one of 44 ft 7 in. diameter in 1888.

From 1866 Spalding was an outstation of Peterborough, which supplied Sturrock and Stirling 0-4-2, 2-4-0 and 0-6-0 types of engines. GNR engines disappeared from Spalding when the Midland and Great Northern Joint Railway engines took over Joint line duties, in February 1895. After the demise of the M&GNJR as seperate entity, in 1936, LNER engines, including many GNR types, once again appeared at Spalding shed, sub-shedded from Peterborough, and under the charge of a foreman fitter from Doncaster.

The shed closed on Monday 7th March, 1960, the turntable being removed the following April, and the shed eventually being demolished.

The first few years of the GNR Company's history saw it without the services of a locomotive superintendent for a considerable period of time. During the first few months Benjamin Cubitt, brother of Joseph, acted as advisor to the company. Upon Cubitt's death, only two years after taking the job, Edward Bury, a friend of Joseph Cubitt, took over in 1846. His position was one of extreme delicacy, in view of his dual capacity as an official of a railway company and a member of a firm of locomotive builders.

It was not until Archibald Sturrock was installed as locomotive engineer, in 1850, that the GNR began to design and eventually build locomotives to its own designs. Prior to this time the company bought locomotives from established manufacturers. The first locomotives to work on the GNR were built by Sharp Brothers and Company of Manchester, Nos. 3 and 4 working the Loop. The Sharps were chosen by Benjamin Cubitt, based on a wide experience of most private makes of engine, during his time as locomotive engineer to the Brighton, Croydon and Dover Railways Joint Locomotive Committee. The Sharps proved

'126' class 0-4-2WT No. 122 at Peterborough on 28th March, 1903. Shedded at Boston in the early 1900s this engine worked the Spilsby branch. It was station pilot at Peterborough during 1915-1916 and withdrawn from Boston in 1918.   *LCGB/Ken Nunn Collection*

Ex-GNR class 'E1' 2-4-0 No. 4070. A Retford engine for most of its life it was one of the last two survivors of its class (the other being No. 3814, of Louth). As No. 1070 it moved to Lincoln shed in 1923 and as late as 19th April, 1926, worked a horse box special from Lincoln to Kings Cross. Withdrawn in June 1924, she was reinstated in July and became LNER No. 4070 in October.
                                                                                     Author's Collection

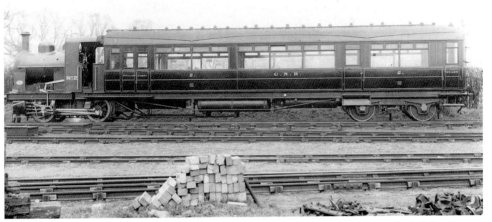

GNR railmotor No. 2, allocated to Lincoln in 1912 and still there in 1918.   *Author's Collection*

GNR class 'A5' No. 261 at Lincoln in 1902. This 4-2-2 was designed by Ivatt for top link express work and built in 1901. No. 261 worked passenger trains over the Loop.

LCGB/Ken Nunn Collection

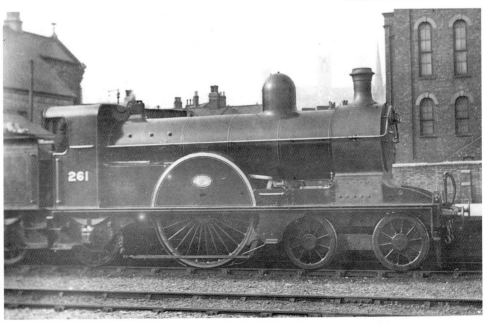

well capable of handling the light slow trains over the level Lincolnshire lines. Fifty of these engines were ordered by the GNR, having 5 ft 6 in. driving wheels, 15 in. x 20 in. inside cylinders and were provided with six-wheel tenders. The price per engine was £1,860 and £460 for each tender.

In 1852 a number of Sharps were converted to tank engines at Boston Works. These engines worked semi-fast trains between Boston and Lincoln, eventually being employed on country branch lines; the Spilsby and Skegness branches were home to the 2-2-2Ts. 0-4-2 tender conversions of the Sharps worked the Boston to Lincoln line during the 1880s.

Following the Sharps came 20 more single wheelers, built by R.W. Hawthorn of Newcastle-on-Tyne, in June 1847. These were that firm's standard design and cost £1,876 for the engine and £380 for the tender. Known as 'Small Hawthorns' they had 6 ft driving wheels and 15 in. x 21 in. cylinders. The 'Small Hawthorns' began work on the Loop line passenger trains between Boston and Peterborough.

Six 0-4-0 goods engines were ordered from Bury, Curtis and Kennedy, at a cost of £1,800 per engine and £300 per tender. They had 5 ft wheels and 15 in. x 24 in. cylinders; Nos. 122-6 were sent to help speed up the completion of the Loop line early in 1848. Six similar engines were ordered from Fairburn's of Manchester.

On 8th November, 1851 Sturrock told the GNR Board that 'two or three tank engines were required for shunting at Lincoln, and Doncaster stations'. Consequently five of the Bury goods engines Nos. 121/2/3/5/6 were converted for this purpose by extending the frames at the rear, and adding a pair of trailing wheels, dispensing with the tenders and adding a saddle tank.

Hawthorn's were instructed to construct 15 goods engines with 5 ft coupled wheels and 15 in. x 24 in. inside cylinders. Prior to Sturrock's first design 31 six-coupled goods locomotives were built by Hawthorn's and Wilson's.

Wilson's 'Jenny Lind' type 2-2-2, Nos. 201/2, worked heavy passenger trains from Boston to York Races during the 1850s.

The '71' class 2-4-0 passenger engines' first duties were to work excursion traffic to and from the 1851 Great Exhibition, in London. The GNR dealt with most of the east coast passengers destined for that event, all of whom travelled through Boston. It was the first time large numbers of passengers had been conveyed by rail and was a real challenge to the GNR. A special savings club was set up in Boston which enabled working class families to visit the exhibition. From May to October excursion trains were run from Boston at least twice a week. On 7th July a train of unprecedented size, 117 short six-wheeled carriages passed through Boston. Although ticket prices were lowered to encourage more people to travel to the exhibition, the extra traffic generated a large amount of revenue.

On 16th October, No. 84, filled with passengers returning home from a day's outing, ran into an empty coal train standing at Kirkstead station. No passengers were hurt but the fireman was seriously injured. The engine sustained considerable damage at the front end. An inquiry established that the collision was caused by 'negligence on the part of parties in charge of signals'.

Many class 'E' 2-4-0 passenger engines spent their last days working

GNR '343' series 0-6-0 No. 4145, at Boston on 29th September, 1926. This engine was built in 1900 and latterly used on local trips and yard shunting duties, it was withdrawn in 1938.

LCGB/Ken Nunn Collection

Boston Loco in LNER days with engine crews in attendance and a class 'D2' on shed.

Author's Collection

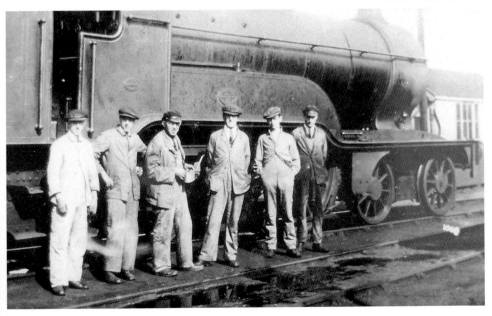

Lincolnshire lines. The last two of the class to survive were No. 814, at Louth, and No. 1070 at Lincoln. No. 1070 was withdrawn in June 1924, but reinstated in July to become LNER No. 4070 in October. The engine worked a horse box special from Lincoln to Kings Cross on 19th April, 1926, and was scrapped in May 1927.

No. 814 also survived to wear LNER black livery as No. 3814, in April 1925, and was the last of its class, withdrawn in November 1927.

By the mid-1890s, Stirling's 7 ft Singles were distributed all over the GNR system, working fast passenger schedules on many secondary routes. Nos. 6, 14, 215 and 222 were shedded at Lincoln, employed on express rosters to and from Grantham for some years. Latterly some of the class were at Peterborough and Boston, working over the Loop. By November 1905 nine engines survived, of which Nos. 4, 39, and 63 were at Boston and No. 222 at Lincoln; these were all 'B5s'. Lincoln also had 'B7s' Nos. 41 and 55.

Class 'F6' 0-2-4WT's Nos. 118A and 122A, both becoming station pilots in 1915-16. At the end of 1916, No. 117A, a Lincoln engine, was withdrawn, Nos. 118A and 122A being withdrawn from Boston in July and November of 1918 respectively.

A high proportion of the survivors of the 0-4-2 mixed traffic tender engine classes 'F2' and 'F3' finished up in Lincolnshire. At the beginning of 1921, Nos, 110A, 200, 326 and 592A were at Peterborough, Nos. 10A, 357, 538A, 551A and 553A at Boston and Nos. 25A, 64A, 104, 575A, 577A, 593A, 951 and 958 at Lincoln.

Intermediate inside-cylindered 7ft 6 in. Singles Nos. 232 and 238 were built in 1885; by 1904 No. 232 was at Lincoln, and used on local duties until withdrawn in June 1906.

Stirling's 'Enlarged' 7 ft 6 in. Singles were shedded at Peterborough in their heyday, from where they worked main line expresses and took part in the 'Races' to Edinburgh in 1888, and Aberdeen in 1895. By April 1905, Peterborough had Nos. 233/7, 874/5 and Boston No. 234. Eight engines survived in 1912, at which time No. 237 was at Peterborough, Nos. 233/3 at Boston and Nos. 235/40 at Lincoln. Many holiday excursions from Leicester to Skegness were worked by ageing 2-2-2's.

By 1912 Stirling's 8 ft Singles, the pride of the GNR main line for over 20 years, were reduced in numbers to seven: Nos. 668, 1001/3/4 at Peterborough and No. 1008 at Lincoln. The latter was sub-shedded at Louth, where it was condemned on 5th June, 1914.

Coal traffic from South Yorkshire was a considerable revenue earner for the GNR. The flatness of the Loop made it ideal for such traffic and kept it away from prestigious main lines. In 1871 Stirling designed a powerful goods engine capable of moving gross loads of 687 tons. Six '174' class engines were built and put into service. However, it was soon realised that space restrictions at Lincoln, (long coal trains were blocking both crossings at once,) and, in certain refuge sidings - there were five between Lincoln and Boston - limited the number of wagons that could be hauled without causing inconvenience. With the reduction in the tonnage of the loads it was possible for standard engines to do the work and thus no further '174' class engines were built.

Class 'D4' 4-4-0 No. 4358 at Boston on 29th September, 1926. This engine was at Boston from 1912 until its withdrawal in 1937 and was often sub-shedded at Wainfleet. In the mid-thirties this duty included passenger trains from Skegness to Firsby and Firsby to Lincoln, plus short runs to Alford and back. *LCGB/Ken Nunn Collection*

Ivatt '1201' series, GNR class 'J14' seen here at Grantham in 1936. Built in 1899 the engine was allocated to Lincoln in 1912 and withdrawn in May 1950. *Author's Collection*

Class 'J4' and 'J5' 0-6-0 goods engines were shedded at Peterborough, Boston and Lincoln throughout their careers. By the time of the 1923 Grouping, 228 engines survived, Peterborough having six 'J4s' and ten 'J5s', Boston eight 'J5s' and Lincoln one 'J4' and nine 'J5s'.

The arrival of the Ivatt class 'C2' 4-4-2Ts, ousted from London by the arrival of Gresleys class 'N2' 0-6-2Ts, saw the end of most of Stirling's 0-4-2 and 0-4-4 tank engines. Class 'C2s' were station pilots at Peterborough North and acted as pilot engines for down express trains when required. Boston engines worked the Spilsby branch. A 'C2' went to Horncastle each weekday morning to work the early branch line trains, before hauling the through London coach over the loop to Boston, where it was attached to the Grimsby to Kings Cross express. This engine returned to Horncastle in the evening with the Kings Cross to Horncastle coach, working back to Boston 'light'.

Steam railcars Nos. 7 and 8 returned from Louth to Lincoln empty at weekends, when repairs were required. Nos. 1, 2, 7 and 8 were allocated to Lincoln. No. 8 was seen several times working Officers' Specials from Lincoln to Skegness via the Loop and the Coningsby Junction to Bellwater Junction line. Regular use of the steam railmotors in the Lincoln area is unclear. After withdrawal of the railcars in 1925-26, the coach portions of each vehicle were converted into articulated Twin Composite Brakes. The modifications involved the conversion of the luggage compartments into passenger accommodation and the rebuilding of the trailing end to include a brake section. The former engine ends were placed together in the centre of the articulated twin, thus placing a brake section at each outer end. The coaches from Nos. 5 and 6, built by the Birmingham Carriage and Wagon Company, became Twin Composite Brake Nos. 44161/2, seating 12 first and 96 thirds, with a length over the buffers of 110 ft 7¼ in. This unit was used on the Horncastle branch, where it lasted until February 1959.

The first carriages to work the GNR were ordered from Walter Williams and were delivered to the East Lincolnshire line. When that line opened in 1848, it had four firsts, two seconds, six thirds and one luggage van.

When Edward Bury took over as locomotive superintendent he thought the carriages from Williams too heavy and expensive. He instructed Williams and Joseph Wright, of Birmingham, to build six vehicles, each to Bury's own specifications. Both firms as well as Brown, Marshall and Company, were awarded substantial orders. The cost of the three classes of vehicle was about £330, £214 and £160 respectively. It is likely that all carriages were finished in varnished teak, this being standard GNR practice by February 1852, although Bury's wife claimed her husband introduced varnished teak as an economy measure.

Sixty ballast wagons were ordered from Neal and Wilson, of Grantham, at a cost of £75 each. Twenty cattle trucks and the same number of sheep trucks were supplied by Ransomes and May, of Ipswich. Sixty open goods wagons were ordered from the same firm on 13th April, 1848, increased to 125 on 25th July. The GNR paid £114 for each of the first 20 and £98 for each of the remainder.

Two guard's brake vans arrived from Joseph Wright on 28th November, 1848.

The GNR shed at Lincoln with its two tiled hipped roofs, each covering two roads. This was GNR standard practice in the 1870s. Ex-GCR class 'C4' Nos. 2902 and 2903, 'B2' No. 1492 and ex-GNR class 'C12' No. 7381 can be seen on shed. *H.C. Casserley*

0-4-0 tram at Peterborough in 1926, the year it was withdrawn from duties in the civil engineer's yard. *LCGB/Ken Nunn Collection*

GNR class 'J19' 0-6-0 No. 3470A at Boston in 1926. No. 3470 here with its rear rods removed, worked at Hall Hills sleeper depot until withdrawn in 1927. Built by Manning, Wardle & Co. in 1863, and virtually completely rebuilt by Stirling in 1872 as a saddle tank.

LCGB/Ken Nunn Collection

Baguley/McEwan Pratt 2 ft 3 in. gauge locomotive, No. 747 of 1918 moving sleeper lengths at Hall Hills sleeper depot, Boston. Originally bought by the War Department Light Railways in 1917, the engine was regauged from 60 cm to 2 ft 3 in. gauge in 1921 and purchased by the GNR for Boston depot. *Author's Collection*

Because of an oversight when contracts were made, Bury had to order six of these vehicles as an urgent priority.

Bury exhibited the prototypes of coal wagons and cattle trucks at Boston, in September 1849, to be viewed by potential manufacturers. Orders were given to Smith and Willey and Ashburys for a total of 650 vehicles.

By the end of 1849, the GNR was equipped with most types of carrying stock, and certainly all the types mentioned would work over the Lincolnshire Loop.

There were some interesting Departmental Stock locomotives used during the life of the Loop. At Peterborough a curious 0-4-0 vertical boilered tank engine was in use from 1908 to 1926, in the Engineer's Yard. A two cylinder vertical engine was geared to one of its axles and the whole enclosed in a box-like metal structure. The engine portion was built at Doncaster in 1892 and used as power for a traverser in the Carriage Works until replaced by electricity. In its turn this engine was replaced by a class 'Y1' Sentinel four-wheeled shunting engine, later No. 4802. This became No. 4992, in March 1937, and remained working at Peterborough until withdrawn as Departmental No. 6, in November 1955. Its previous numbers had been 8133, (1946) and 68133 (1948).

A small building housed the shunting engine used at Hall Hills Sleeper Depot, at Boston. No. 470 was a 0-6-0 standard pattern Manning, Wardle side tank engine, built for the West Yorkshire Railway, in 1863, at which period it was named *Marquis*. Stirling rebuilt the engine so thoroughly in 1872, that it was virtually indistinguishable from his class 'J19' saddle tank shunting engines. It was regarded as a new engine and given the Doncaster Works number 92, although retaining its running number, 470. In 1914 it was equipped to burn oil fuel, supplied from a 200 gallon tank located in the bunker space; at the same time its rear coupling rods were removed, making it an 0-4-2. It remained so until its demise. Transferred to the duplicate list in 1919, 470A was put into Service Stock on 19th December, 1921, for use at Hall Hills, where it remained until its withdrawal on 9th April, 1927. Between 23rd October, 1924 and 10th January, 1925 the engine had a general repair at Doncaster, reappearing painted black with red lining and lettered 'LNER 3470A'.

In November 1926 3470A's duties were taken over by a new Sentinel class 'Y1' shunting engine, No. 4801 (later 4991). this engine was itself replaced at Hall Hills on 9th February, 1940 by class 'Y3' No. 49, which was transferred to Service Stock on 9th April, 1940.

Hall Hills also had 2 ft 3 in. narrow gauge lines within the complex. This system was operated by a Baguley/McEwan Pratt petrol 0-6-0 locomotive, originally ordered by the War Department Light Railways, on 14th February, 1917. Despatched to Calais it ran as LR 284, a 60 cm gauge 10 hp engine. It was regauged by Baguley to 2 ft 3 in. in 1921 and was purchased by the GNR to work at Hall Hills.

A Ruston & Hornsby 0-4-0 standard design (Works No. 202005) was ordered by the LNER in February 1940. Powered by a diesel engine it developed 20 hp at 1200 rpm and was allocated to Hall Hills to work the narrow gauge system.

A Sheffield bound train at Stixwould station in August 1970.   *P. Grey*

The last fisherman's excursion leaving Woodhall Junction for Sheffield in 1969. The photograph taken from the flyover bridge which replaced the old swing bridge seen on the right.

P. Newton

Chapter Eleven

Closure

The decimation of the railways of Lincolnshire began with Dr Beeching's 'rationalisation' proposals in 1963. The Loop line between Coningsby Junction, (the junction for the 'New Line' to Bellwater Junction), and Boston was closed to passengers and freight on 17th June, 1963. The reason offered by British Railways was that the projected expenditure of £72,000, required on trackwork and signalling, was not justified by traffic levels. With the closure of this section of the Loop line the stations at Langrick, Dogdyke and Tattershall closed completely.

The line from Coningsby Junction to Bellwater Junction (on the East Lincolnshire line) saw an increase of traffic as a result of the closure. Coningsby took over as a railhead for areas previously served by Tattershall and Dogdyke stations, as well as becoming the terminus for some trains from Lincoln. This Indian summer was however, short lived, and on 7th October, 1968 the stations along the Coningsby to Bellwater Junction line became unstaffed halts. By 1970 Tumby Woodside was the terminus, dealing with three trains each way daily from Lincoln, the remainder of the line served by four Lincoln to Firsby trains and three in the opposite direction. Coningsby to Bellwater Junction closed on 5th October, 1970 and the removal of the track was completed by May 1972.

On the remainder of the Loop between Boston and Lincoln, the stations at Southrey and Stixwould closed completely on 5th October, 1970. On this date many services over much of the East Lincolnshire main line were also lost. With the closing of these stations a chapter of rural railway history disappeared, a slice of GNR heritage which had survived and largely retained many of the early features of that company.

Goods traffic to Bardney remained, to serve the sugar beet factory. Woodhall Junction survived, allowing access to the Horncastle branch. This was by now a freight only line, operated by an '08' class diesel locomotive from Lincoln. This arrangement prevailed until closure of the branch to Horncastle on 5th April, 1971, which also saw the end of Woodhall Junction goods yard.

Only the line to Bardney now remained. This was run as a private siding. Malcolm Roughley visited the line on 23rd May, 1980, and described his experience as follows:

At 09.17 I arrived in Lincoln Central and met Inspector D. Coxon of the Doncaster Division; we made our way to Holmes yard, which is the freight centre for Lincoln, but today sees little traffic. At one time Lincoln could boast the existence of four engine sheds, Great Northern, Great Central, Great Eastern and Midland Railways, and , located at the crossroads of the railway network in the country, the city saw heavy traffic in coal, cattle, grain, fruit, potatoes and sugar beet. Today there is only one mandatory freight working which leaves Lincoln for general traffic and this is the return 06.15 ex-Tinsley Yard, apart from the conditional 'trips as required' down the Bardney branch. Standing on an adjacent line in the yard was 03034, one of six '03s' allocated to Lincoln. Four of these smart little Gardner shunters are stationed at Lincoln, while the other two are sub-shedded at Boston.

On one of the through roads 08101 vibrated noisily at the head of a train of 16 coal wagons, with a brake van at both ends. Built in 1954, this rather grimy looking member of the ubiquitous '08' class was preparing to stretch its legs, as it were, and although limited to an engine speed of 15 mph, was ready to trundle the ten miles to Bardney to deliver coal to the sugar factory there. I was quite surprised to see the '08' rostered for branch line work, but as there are no main line locomotives allocated to Lincoln, the '08s' and '03s' share the work between them. Anything above a 900 ton load requires a double trip, but trains rarely exceed this weight. I clambered aboard the locomotive and at 11.20 received a 'dolly' [signal] for exit onto the running lines, we trundled over the High Street level crossing, still a major cause of irritation to local motorists, and through the limits of Lincoln Central.

The crossing gates which once guarded Pelham Street have gone, now replaced by a flyover for the road traffic, we rocked and swayed through the crossover, the diagonal of which is the main Grimsby to Newark line, past Sincil Bank signal box and the large diesel railcar depot and thence onto the Sleaford line. This ex-GN & GE Joint route is the mainstay of the East Anglia traffic and there is a considerable amount of freight traffic along this stretch originating from Whitemoor Yard in March. Trailing in, from the right, comes the avoiding line from Pyewipe Junction, which, together with the divergence of the Bardney branch, forms Greetwell Junction. The avoiding line to Pyewipe Junction is mainly used by through freight trains which do not need to stop at Holmes Yard for traffic purposes or crew changes, and the occasional passenger trains to and from East Anglia (though the Eastern Region is proposing withdrawal of this facility).

We slowed to walking pace as we approached the box, for it was here that we were to accept the staff, which would give us authority to traverse the branch. The staff was, in effect, a shortened piece of wooden brake handle, upon which was nailed a rectangular aluminium plate with the words, 'Greetwell Jct. to Bardney' inscribed.

We were now on the branch proper and working on the principle of 'one engine in steam', or 'one train working'. We had, in reality, taken possession of the branch, and no other working by any other train was possible. The staff would have to be returned to the signal box at Greetwell by hand if, in the event of a failure, another engine was required to assist.

The line here is on a sharply falling gradient away from the Sleaford line and, after about a third of a mile, we approached the site of Washingborough Junction, which was originally another connection made with the Lincoln to Sleaford line nearby the present diesel depot. Nothing remains of the junction now except for a few rusty sections of rail and the station of Washingborough, some few hundred yards further on, where both platforms are in existence together with the station house which is privately occupied. The line now runs on the level alongside the River Witham to the north and a drain cut to the south. In exceptionally wet weather the water has been known to lap against the sleepers of the track. A further five miles brought us to the site of Five Mile House station, once a wooden sleepered halt with a small siding for potato traffic, but today no trace remains.

Our objective, the large rectangular-looking factory owned by the British Sugar Corporation, at Bardney, could now be seen, although we were still some four miles distant. Indeed, the structure can be seen from Lincoln, as can the cathedral of that city be observed from Bardney. The line, originally double track, was noticeably rusty, as the last train along the branch had been the weed killer unit some five weeks before, with precious little traffic before that. The freight service to Bardney is classed as a trip working, and runs as required on Mondays, Wednesdays and Fridays only. During the close season, which is from February to October, the only traffic of any significance is the coal which is taken to the factory and stockpiled in readiness for the sugar beet season, which begins in the autumn.

After some 50 minutes running time from Lincoln, we slowly eased over the bridge

Demolition train at Woodhall Junction seen from the Horncastle branch bay. The once splendid station nameboard has been replaced by a much abbreviated version. *P. Newton*

Coningsby Junction and signal box on 27th October, 1970, the trackbed of the Boston-Lincoln line is seen to the right. *R.B. Wilkinson*

and negotiated the severe reverse curve, which announces one's arrival at Bardney. The Bardney distant signal was still apparent, a genuine GN lower quadrant somersault on a faded lattice post. Trailing in from the left, on a shallow embankment, I could observe the track bed of the one-time rural branch to Louth via Wragby and Donington-on-Bain. The level crossing gates, which span the road, were unlocked by a key, which was housed in the station buildings at Bardney, still in remarkable condition and quite spotless inside. The key for the station itself is brought down with the staff by the guard from Greetwell Junction. I was surprised to find the station much as it would have been, with the nameboard in Eastern Region blue, planted firmly on the island platform, and a variety of lineside signs of GNR and LNER origin proliferating around the level crossing. The line becomes double track through the station and continues towards Boston in a long straight for a half a mile until the entrance to the factory is reached. A trailing connection to the right, operated by a ground frame, leads back into the extensive sidings, comprising some eight roads, and a further spur which runs round to the rear of the factory.

The '08' having dropped its load, came fussing out of the yard with the brake vans and halted at the end of the island platform while the staff gathered for a tea break. By 13.00 we were ready for the 'right away', and, after proceeding gingerly through the gates, the little '08' picked up speed to 15 mph and swayed along towards Lincoln, allowing me fine views of the surrounding district through the large rear cab windows; herons and grebes seemed to be the most common sights. We received a through line at Greetwell and ran on to the main line leaving the strange staff with the signalman, and the 'one engine in steam' branch to resume its slumber until the beet season would begin in earnest.

The arrangement described above survived until final closure of the branch. In 1983 the last remains of the Boston-Lincoln section between Bardney and Lincoln was lifted. Although closure of the branch relieved British Rail of the expense of maintaining Greetwell Junction signal box, in Lincoln, the decision was taken against the wishes of the British Sugar Corporation.

The present day Peterborough station is on the site of the old Peterborough North. When Peterborough East station closed all trains went through Peterborough North. The station was reconstructed between 1972 and 1974 and provided with modest functional buildings and four through platforms. To the east of the station the Great Northern Hotel has recently been expanded. New England loco depot closed in 1969.

Three miles north of Peterborough station, at Werrington Junction, the line to Spalding heads off in a north-easterly direction. Spalding station is a pathetic shadow of its former self, linked to Peterborough in one direction, and to Doncaster and Retford in the other.

The Lincoln-Gainsborough section of the loop survives, as part of the Doncaster to Peterborough connection. Only Saxilby station survives between Lincoln Central and Gainsborough Lea Road.

Lincoln Central has done well out of modernisation, the station building enjoying a £20,000 face lift, as well as gaining the traffic from the former St Marks station by means of a £1.7 million link line over a curve near Boultham Junction.

It is indeed an odd reflection on so-called 'progress' when one considers the small villages along the River Witham that once enjoyed regular and reliable public transport services, firstly by river and later by rail. Nowadays if they are lucky, they are served by the occasional market bus.

Diesel shunter No. 08 101 stands at the end of the Bardney branch as the remaining spur of the former GNR Loop Line was known by this time, May 1980.   *Malcolm Roughley*

Flower Festival special IZ40 ex-Tonbridge, class '47' No. 47 583 alongside diesel shunter No. 08 102 at the north end of Spalding station on 7th May, 1983.   *Horace Gamble*

'Deltic' class No. 55 005 *The Prince of Wales's Own Regiment of Yorkshire* is about to cross the River Witham at Lincoln. The engine is hauling the diverted 'Flying Scotsman' which had been routed over the former GN&GE Joint line, 23rd April, 1978. *Rev. Graham B. Wise*

Appendix One

The GN & GE Joint Railway

The Great Eastern Railway had ambitions to reach the south Yorkshire coalfield through Lincolnshire, thus gaining access to the North. These aspirations however, put it in direct competition with the ambitious and wealthier GNR.

As early as 1864, the GER had entered an agreement with the Lancashire and Yorkshire Railway, to run a line from Askern, near Doncaster, by way of Lincoln and Peterborough to Long Stanton, in Cambridgeshire. This would have given the L&YR access to London through Liverpool Street station. After fierce opposition from the GNR, the Bill was rejected on its second reading on 14th March, 1865.

In 1863 a Bill proposed to extend the line from Spalding to March, a kind of 'tit for tat' exchange. Both proposals were acceptable to both companies, providing running rights could be agreed.

The GNR also proposed extending its Lincolnshire Loop line to Doncaster, thus cutting out the run over the MS&LR line from Sykes Junction to Retford. With this section in place the whole route from March via Boston to Doncaster was possible. The GNR offerred the GER running powers, for mineral traffic only, between Spalding and Doncaster. This did not satisfy the GER, who wanted direct links with the south Yorkshire coalfield. Their proposal was that the two companies should build a loop running between Spalding, Gainsborough and Doncaster, which would be jointly owned.

At this point all appeared to be moving smoothly, with the two companies set to build a new line from Spalding to Lincoln. The GER, however, were experiencing financial problems of such a degree that the shareholders replaced the Directors, the newcomers blocking all joint line proposals.

Consultations began again in 1872, with no success. In 1878 the GER revised its earlier scheme to link with the L&YR. This greatly annoyed the GNR, who put forward their own proposal for a direct line from Spalding to Lincoln via Sleaford, suggesting that the joint line should start at Huntingdon. The GER objected, taking the matter to Parliament, where it lost the debate.

Finally the GNR's Spalding-Lincoln plans were approved, in exchange for the GER being allowed to have running powers to Doncaster. Agreement was at last achieved in 1879, when the Joint Line Bill proposed a system of lines running from Huntingdon to Black Carr Junction, near Doncaster, via St Ives, March, Spalding, Sleaford, Lincoln and Gainsborough. The whole to be managed by a committee of five Directors from each company, which came into being on 3rd July, 1879. At this point the Lincoln, Gainsborough and Doncaster section of the GNR Loop line became part of the responsibility of the GN & GE Joint Railway, which opened in 1882.

There was only one section of railway constructed under the new proposals, namely that between Spalding and Lincoln. The rest of the system comprised lines already in existence, and which were merely transferred to the new Joint Line committee.

One important outcome of the emergence of the new Joint Line was the construction of the Lincoln avoiding line which ran to the south and west of the city. The high level line allowed freight traffic a clear run free from level crossings.

A connecting line between the GNR Loop line and the avoiding line ran between Washingborough Junction and Greetwell Junction. It was double track and a mile long, running entirely on embankment and viaduct. The steepest gradient was 1 in 122 and the sharpest curve had a radius of 15 chains. Built by Baker and Firbank the connecting line was to be worked and maintained by the GNR. The viaduct was 75 yards long, had three 50 ft openings, and was supported on cast iron piers. Problems with the foundations, caused by the boggy nature of the ground upon which they were constructed, precipitated the closing of the line for repairs between 25th May, 1884 and 20th July, 1885.

Hudswell, Clarke 0-6-0ST No. 1604 of 1928 seen here on site at Bardney sugar factory on Sunday, 21st April, 1974. *Horace Gamble*

The Hudswell, Clarke's replacement was this 0-4-0 Ruston diesel engine seen here at the Bardney factory in the late 1970s. *Author's Collection*

Appendix Two

British Sugar Corporation Sidings
at Bardney

The sugar factory at Bardney opened in 1927. The entrance to the factory sidings was about half a mile south of Bardney station on the down side of the main line. A trailing connection, operated by a ground frame, led into the extensive sidings, which comprised some eight roads with a spur which ran to various points in the factory system. The sidings, in fact, formed a continuous run-round, emerging again as a single line back at the station, to rejoin the Lincoln line.

British Sugar Corporation had its own shunting engine. Hudswell, Clarke 0-6-0ST No. 1604 of 1928 worked there until replaced by an 0-4-0 Ruston diesel shunter, built in Lincoln, which worked through until the rail system closed and the track was lifted in 1983. No. 1604 is preserved by Alan Turner at the Lincolnshire Railway Museum, at Burgh-le-Marsh. The engines would marshall the vans and take them to the boilers. Because of the extent of the sidings shunting operations were not difficult.

When the harvest of beet was in season the factory was in operation continuously for about three or four months, depending upon the strength of the crop. Rail traffic also increased accordingly. During the beet season, a shunter was employed at Bardney each day, otherwise he would accompany the guard on the train when it ran. Maurice Clarke was head shunter at Bardney station from 1958 to the last train. His son-in-law, Mike Rogers, of Bardney, described train movements at Bardney:

In the early 1960s steam locomotives working the 'block' trains included class '02', '04', 'K1' and 'B16'. These worked directly to Doncaster for onward transit to Scotland, where the pulp was used as animal feed.

Traffic for the sugar factory originated mainly from Tumby Woodside, Eastville Little Steeping, Thorpe Culvert, Wainfleet and Sibsey. The empty wagons were made up from empty coal wagons from the factory, or 're-using' emptied sugar beet wagons. These were mainly unfitted 12 ton wooden vehicles, latterly 16 ton steel mineral wagons were used. The empty wagons were sent to Woodhall Spa on the afternoon Boston pick-up goods rather than on the first Lincoln Firsby pick-up in the morning, which would have been overloaded to Woodhall. This pick-up brought cans for J. Morrell & Co. in vanfits, plus the transhipment vans for the Woodhall Spa lorries and the Horncastle traffic, New Line vehicles being left at Woodhall. Upon return, New Line traffic plus the mineral empties were removed at around 9.30 am. Coal for the sugar factory was taken to Holmes yard, in Lincoln, by the Bardney Pilot, which arrived at about 11.00 am. The coal was left at the south end of the sugar factory sidings, after which the pilot shunted Morrell's sidings at midday. Engine power was usually a class 'J11' 0-6-0 from Lincoln shed, later a Standard class '4MT'. The load was often 20 wagons of washed singles in 16 ton mineral wagons, from Bilsthorpe Colliery, occasionally Blidworth.

The third pick-up arrived at midday, a Boston engine bringing a mixture, but usually not a lot of traffic for Bardney. However if there were problems on the East Lincolnshire line, beet traffic could make 15 or so wagons.

A fourth pick-up, running Lincoln to Boston, was, as far as Bardney was concerned, a 'back up' to the mid-morning trip. Any coal, maybe 10 or so, empty wagons (vanfits) for pulp and any coke for the sugar factory, this was an odd wagon now and then.

The late afternoon return trip from the New Line reversed some 8 to 10 sugar beet wagons into the north end of the factory sidings. Any surplus coal wagons were taken to Lincoln by returning pilot, this was sometimes just before the New Line train arrived and sometimes just after. The pilot usually filled up with pulp wagons for Lincoln Holmes, many going on to Appleby and Kirkby Stephen on the Settle and Carlisle line.

The 'block' trains usually departed between 11.00 am and 1.00 pm. This was always an achievement because the drivers were not able to get a good run out of the sidings and fought to get the train up the incline and over the bridge, half a mile away, the engines often working nearly to a stop.

The make up of the pick-ups in 1958:

(arr.)

7.00 am	Lincoln-Firsby	Class 'J39'	0-6-0	No. 64741
11.00 am	Lincoln-Bardney	Class 'J15'	0-6-0	Nos. 64315/18
12.00 noon	Boston-Lincoln	Class 'J6'	0-6-0	Nos. 64190/81
		Class 'A5'	4-6-2T	No. 69808
3.30 pm	Firsby-Lincoln	as above (7.00 am)		
4.30-5.15 pm	Boston-Lincoln	Class 'K2'	2-6-0	Nos. 61761/42

This view of Bardney sugar factory taken on 14th June, 1958, shows the Hudswell, Clarke No. 1604 with the Ruston diesel partially hidden in the background.   *John R. Bonsor*

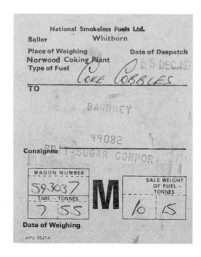

Appendix Three

J. Morrell & Company Siding
at Bardney

Messrs J. Morrell was a canning company based at Bardney and situated alongside the Boston-Lincoln line to the west of Bardney station. Access to its siding was from the branch which ran from Bardney to Louth.

The siding usually held 18 vanfits and one or two mineral wagons for coal delivery. There were seven positions for unloading empty cans, which were usually sent daily from the Metal Box Company, at Wisbech. Sometimes special 'Red Heart' dog food cans were sent from the Metal Box Company, at Worcester, these came in 'Shockfits'.

To make things easy for positioning, 11 empty vanfits were shunted in, these were used for loading as required by the factory. Two shunts were completed each day, at 12.00 noon and at 6.00. The midday shunt was most critical as it had to fit into the factory lunchtime. It was mostly a case of replacing the empty can wagons for the afternoons work. The evening shunt included the loaded wagons of canned vegetables and dog food.

There were two spaces between the vanfits under the loading canopy and the coal hopper. When there were two coal wagons in the siding, the empty wagon was pinched or pushed along to allow the second wagon access to the hopper. These wagons were emptied by hand.

To gain some idea of the importance of the midday shunt, on occasion a 'Britannia' class locomotive, running light from New England to Immingham, was diverted to do the work. Mike Rogers remembers seeing *John of Gaunt* on such duties. Indeed the route availability of the siding was group 8.

For safety reasons a key was obtained from the signalman, subject to the Louth line being clear. The key was inserted into a box and turned, (key position 1 on the plan) thus activating the bell system, which warned everyone of the shunt about to take place. The shunter walked along the 'gantry' to check wagon doors and that factory staff were clear of the siding. He then made his way to the ground frame and inserted the key, (No. 2 on the plan) to activate the points for the siding. The ground frame could not be operated without the above procedure being completed. After the shunt the procedure was reversed.

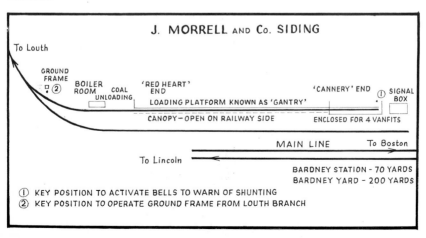

Dedication

For my wife, Jane, whose Great Grandfather, Frederick Clark, worked engines over the GNR Lincolnshire Loop line.

References and Acknowledgements

The History of the Great Northern Railway by C.H. Grinling (Metheun, 1898)
The Great Northern Railway by John Wrottesley (Batsford, 1979)
The Great Northern Railway by O.S. Nock (Ian Allan, 1958)
Great Northern Railway Supplement, *The Engineer*, 28th November, 1913
Great Northern Locomotive History (RCTS 1986-92)
Great Northern Railway Engine Sheds by Griffiths & Hooper (Irwell Press, 1989)
The Railway History of Lincoln by Ruddock & Pearson (Ruddock, 1985)
Boston a Railway Town by Cartwright & Walker (KMS, 1987)
History of the Fens of South Lincolnshire by W.H. Wheeler 1896.
Lincolnshire Towns and Industry 1700-1914 by Neil Wright, 1982
The Victorian Peasant by Richard Heath (Alan Sutton, 1989)
The Lincolnshire Potato Railways by Stewart Squires (The Oakwood Press, 1987)
The East Lincolnshire Railway by A.J. Ludlam (The Oakwood Press, 1991)
The Louth to Bardney Branch by A.J. Ludlam & W.B. Herbert (The Oakwood Press, 1984)
The Horncastle and Woodhall Junction Railway by A.J. Ludlam (The Oakwood Press, 1986)
Picture Post, 24th December, 1949
The Lincolnshire Chronicle
The Illustrated London News
The Lincolnshire Archives
Lincoln Central Reference Library
The Great Northern Railway Society
The Public Record Office, Kew

Individuals who have helped include: Michael Back, Percy Carter, Norman Clark, Jim Cuthbert, John Edgington, Peter Holmes of the Gresley Society, Colin Judge, Maurice Knight, Patrick Newton, J.G. Porter, David Robinson, Michael Rogers, Charles Sharp, and many others; thanks to you all.